CRITICAL THINKING
SKILLS SUCCESS
IN 20 MINUTES A DAY

OTHER TITLES OF INTEREST FROM LEARNINGEXPRESS

Biology Success in 20 Minutes a Day

Chemistry Success in 20 Minutes a Day

Earth Science Success in 20 Minutes a Day

Grammar Success in 20 Minutes a Day, 2nd Edition

Physics Success in 20 Minutes a Day

Practical Math Success in 20 Minutes a Day, 3rd Edition

Reading Comprehension Success in 20 Minutes a Day, 4th Edition

Reasoning Skills Success in 20 Minutes a Day, 3rd Edition

Statistics Success in 20 Minutes a Day

Trigonometry Success in 20 Minutes a Day

Vocabulary and Spelling Success in 20 Minutes a Day, 5th Edition

Writing Skills Success in 20 Minutes a Day, 4th Edition

CRITICAL THINKING SKILLS SUCCESS

IN 20 MINUTES A DAY

2nd Edition

LEARNINGEXPRESS®

NEW YORK

Library of Congress Cataloging-in-Publication Data:
Starkey, Lauren B., 1962–
    Critical thinking skills success / Lauren Starkey.—2nd ed.
        p. cm.
    Rev. ed. of: Critical thinking skills success in 20 minutes a day / Lauren Starkey.
    Includes bibliographical references and index.
    1. Critical thinking—Handbooks, manuals, etc. I. Starkey, Lauren B., 1962- Critical
    thinking skills success in 20 minutes a day. II. LearningExpress (Organization)
    LB1590.3.S73 2010
    160—dc22   2009033340

Printed in the United States of America

9 8 7 6 5 4 3 2

Second Edition

ISBN 978-1-57685-726-7

For more information or to place an order, contact LearningExpress at:
    2 Rector Street
    26th Floor
    New York, NY 10006

Or visit us at:
    www.learnatest.com

Contents

CONTENTS

HOW TO USE THIS BOOK ▶

Critical Thinking Skills Success in 20 Minutes a Day is all about helping you think about the way you think. That's called *metacognition,* translated as "knowing about knowing" and meaning "to have knowledge of your own thoughts and the things that influence your thinking." Sound complicated? It's not, especially when you learn how lesson by lesson, just 20 minutes at a time.

Critical thinkers approach a complicated situation with awareness of their thoughts, beliefs, and opinions, and how to direct them rationally. In addition, critical thinkers are willing to explore, question, and search for solutions to problems. All those skills add up to greater success at school, on the job, and at home. Colleges, universities, and many employers have identified critical thinking as a measure of how well someone will do in school or in the workplace. So, college entrance exams include critical-thinking sections, and many employers, including the government, administer exams, like the California or Cornell Critical Thinking Tests, to job applicants.

Generally, critical thinking involves both problem solving and reasoning, terms often used interchangeably. More specifically, critical thinking includes the ability to:

- make observations.
- listen attentively to others.
- recognize and define problems.
- be curious, ask relevant questions, and use multiple resources to find facts.
- challenge and examine beliefs, assumptions, and opinions.
- assess the validity of statements and arguments.
- know the difference between logical and illogical arguments.
- make wise decisions and judgments.
- find valid solutions.

Each lesson in this book explains a specific critical-thinking skill, and then lets you practice using that skill. Here's exactly what you'll find:

- Lessons 1 and 2 explain how to recognize and define problems. You'll practice prioritizing problems and spotting an actual problem versus its symptoms and/or consequences.
- Lesson 3 deals with how to be a better observer of situations around you. This will help you make logical inferences, a key critical-thinking skill that you'll practice using.
- Lessons 4 and 5 explore how graphic organizers can help you organize ideas and set goals. You will practice using these visual tools to lead from problems to solutions.
- Lesson 6 covers troubleshooting, the ability to spot difficulties that could interfere with your problem-solving goals. You'll practice removing setbacks before they happen to keep you on track for success.
- Lessons 7 and 8 explain where and how to find information to help you make wise decisions. You'll discover how to evaluate facts and figures to assure that they're accurate. This is especially important when using websites, which may have biased, misleading, or incorrect information.
- Lesson 9 covers the art of persuasion. You'll learn how to recognize persuasion when it is being used on you—and how to use it effectively yourself!
- Lesson 10 is about statistics and how they're often manipulated. You'll see what makes a survey valid and how to spot one that's invalid.
- Lesson 11 looks at the effect of emotions on critical thinking. Knowing how to keep your emotional responses in check is important to clear thinking.

- Lessons 12 and 13 explain deductive reasoning, one of two kinds of logic. You'll practice spotting the difference between valid and invalid deduction, which can lead to illogical ideas.
- Lessons 14 and 15 are about inductive reasoning, the other kind of logic. You'll discover how to make a valid inductive argument, and how induction is misused to create illogical conclusions.
- Lesson 16 covers how people intentionally misuse logical arguments to distract you from a real problem. You'll practice seeking out such distractions.
- Lesson 17 deals with judgment calls, those difficult decisions you have to make when there's no clear-cut right or wrong answer. Practicing how to calculate risks and consequences can help you make solid judgment calls.
- Lesson 18 explains how important it is to know the difference between an explanation and an argument. You'll practice telling them apart.
- Lesson 19 covers the kinds of critical-thinking questions used on exams for school admissions and employment. You'll practice answering some questions like those you will find on tests.
- Lesson 20 reviews all that you've read. This gives you a valuable quick-reference tool to use as a refresher anytime.

You may already be good at implementing some critical-thinking skills, but need help with others. So before you start, take the pretest that follows to find out how much you already know and what you need to work on. At the end of the book, there's a posttest to assess how much your skills have improved. For now, let's get started with that pretest. Good luck!

ADDITIONAL ONLINE PRACTICE ▶

Whether you need help building basic skills or preparing for an exam, visit the LearningExpress Practice Center! On this site, you can access additional practice materials. Using the code below, you'll be able to log in and answer additional critical-thinking practice questions. This online practice will also provide you with:

- **Immediate scoring**
- **Detailed answer explanations**
- **Personalized recommendations for further practice and study**

Log in to the LearningExpress Practice Center by using this URL: **www.learnatest.com/practice**

This is your Access Code: **7267**

Follow the steps online to redeem your access code. After you've used your access code to register with the site, you will be prompted to create a username and password. For easy reference, record them here:

Username: _____ **Password:**_____

With your username and password, you can log in and answer these practice questions as many times as you like. If you have any questions or problems, please contact LearningExpress customer service at 1-800-295-9556 ext. 2, or e-mail us at **customerservice@learningexpressllc.com**.

PRETEST ▶

This pretest is designed to help you figure out how much you already know about critical-thinking skills. You may find that you know more than you think you do, because you use these skills in day-to-day living. You may discover that many questions on the test are easy to answer, but there could be some you find more difficult. This will help you pinpoint any skills you need to work on.

The test has 30 multiple-choice questions. If this is your book, fill in the circle of each correct answer on the following answer sheet. If the book isn't yours, list the numbers 1–30 on a piece of paper and write your answers there. Take as much time as you need to finish the test, and then check your answers on the answer key at the end. Each answer lists which lesson in the book covers the concept(s) in that question. Pay particular attention to any lesson that you chose an incorrect answer for as you work through the book.

1.	(a)	(b)	(c)	(d)
2.	(a)	(b)	(c)	(d)
3.	(a)	(b)	(c)	(d)
4.	(a)	(b)	(c)	(d)
5.	(a)	(b)	(c)	(d)
6.	(a)	(b)	(c)	(d)
7.	(a)	(b)	(c)	(d)
8.	(a)	(b)	(c)	(d)
9.	(a)	(b)	(c)	(d)
10.	(a)	(b)	(c)	(d)

11.	(a)	(b)	(c)	(d)
12.	(a)	(b)	(c)	(d)
13.	(a)	(b)	(c)	(d)
14.	(a)	(b)	(c)	(d)
15.	(a)	(b)	(c)	(d)
16.	(a)	(b)	(c)	(d)
17.	(a)	(b)	(c)	(d)
18.	(a)	(b)	(c)	(d)
19.	(a)	(b)	(c)	(d)
20.	(a)	(b)	(c)	(d)

21.	(a)	(b)	(c)	(d)
22.	(a)	(b)	(c)	(d)
23.	(a)	(b)	(c)	(d)
24.	(a)	(b)	(c)	(d)
25.	(a)	(b)	(c)	(d)
26.	(a)	(b)	(c)	(d)
27.	(a)	(b)	(c)	(d)
28.	(a)	(b)	(c)	(d)
29.	(a)	(b)	(c)	(d)
30.	(a)	(b)	(c)	(d)

1. You conducted a successful job search, and now have three offers from which to choose. What can you do to most thoroughly investigate your potential employers? (Choose all that apply.)
   a. check out their websites
   b. watch the news to see if the companies are mentioned
   c. research their financial situations
   d. speak with people who work for them already

2. Which is NOT an example of a persuasion technique?
   a. "If you care about the environment, and who doesn't, give generously to our Save the Mongoose Fund today!"
   b. "I've been eating Wheat-O's cereal since I was a kid," says super-athlete Mark Guyerman. "They give me energy to win . . . and they'll do the same for you!"
   c. Soft-Sole Sneakers for toddlers are available at Murphy's Discount Store.
   d. "Send me to Washington as your senator if you want things done. I'll stop all the government waste!"

3. Choose the best conclusion for an argument that begins, "The other members of Philip's swim team . . ."
   a. won their events, so Philip will win his event, too.
   b. have been swimming for at least six years, so Philip has been swimming for six years, too.
   c. prefer to swim in outdoor pools, so Philip prefers outdoor pools, too.
   d. wear swim trunks with the school logo on them, so Philip wears them, too.

4. Marcy's American Lit teacher gives a quiz every Monday on the 50 pages of reading he assigns on Fridays. His quizzes are becoming harder as the semester progresses, and Marcy hasn't been doing very well on them. What can she do to troubleshoot the problem and hopefully get better grades on the quizzes?
   a. plan to get to class early on Monday to skim the pages
   b. look for a new outfit to wear on Monday so she'll be relaxed
   c. set aside time on Sunday to read and review the new material
   d. spend an hour on Saturday looking over what she missed on past quizzes

5. Which is NOT a sound argument?
   a. Sabrina wanted to be a better figure skater, so she took extra lessons and practiced every day. Her skating improved so much that she entered a competition.
   b. Yesterday, a black cat ran in front of me, and later, I lost my wallet. If I don't see that black cat today, I won't have any bad luck.
   c. We had a storm last night with hurricane-strength winds, and many trees were downed. There was a citywide power outage.
   d. On a clear day, I can see the top of Murphy Monument from my house. If it's clear tomorrow, I'll be able to see the monument.

6. You are trying to decide what kind of car to buy. You make a chart to compare a two-seater sports car, a two-door sedan, and a minivan in three categories. Which would NOT be a suitable category?
   a. price
   b. gas mileage
   c. tire pressure
   d. storage capacity

7. Which scenario best represents a situation that has been decided by emotion alone?
   a. Sue hates the winter, so even though she can't afford it, she takes a vacation to the Bahamas.
   b. The school shuts down after a bomb threat.
   c. Third-quarter earnings for Marie's company were much higher than predicted.
   d. Alexis needs a new mixer, so she watches the newspaper ads and buys one when it goes on sale.

8. When would it be better to do research in the library rather than on the Internet?
   a. You are writing a report on recent U. S. Supreme Court decisions.
   b. You want to know the historical performance of a stock you are considering purchasing.
   c. You need to compare credit card interest rates.
   d. You want to find out more about the old trails through the forest in your town.

9. You read a story in the newspaper about salary negotiations with public transportation workers. The workers are threatening to go on strike tomorrow if their demands for higher wages and better benefits are not met. What can you infer from this news story?
   a. Health insurance premiums are very expensive.
   b. The cost of gas will make ticket prices increase in the next few weeks.
   c. People who ride the bus should look for possible alternative transportation.
   d. Employers never like to meet salary demands.

10. What is wrong with this argument?

"You think we need a new regulation to control air pollution? I think we already have too many regulations. Politicians just love to pass new ones, and control us even more than they already do. It is suffocating. We definitely do not need any new regulations!"

   a. The person speaking doesn't care about the environment.
   b. The person speaking has changed the subject.
   c. The person speaking is running for political office.
   d. The person speaking does not understand pollution.

11. What should you NOT rely on when making a judgment call?
   a. intuition
   b. common sense
   c. gossip
   d. past experience

12. Which is NOT a valid argument?
   a. There are six cans of tomatoes in Carlo's pantry and 14 in his basement. There are no other cans of tomatoes in his house. Therefore, he has 20 cans of tomatoes in his house.
   b. Everyone northbound on the Interstate yesterday was late to work. Faith was northbound on the Interstate. Faith was late to work.
   c. Huang lives in either Kansas City, Kansas, or Kansas City, Missouri. If he lives in Kansas, then he is an American.
   d. No one who eats in the cafeteria likes the pizza. My boss eats in the cafeteria. Therefore, my boss not like the pizza.

13. Mia wants to go to London, Paris, and Rome for vacation next year. She found a tour to the three cities advertised online for only $2,000, but she has just $750 in her savings account. Which is Mia's best goal-setting strategy?
  a. plan a shorter, cheaper trip to just one country in Europe
  b. set up a website asking people to donate money to help pay for the trip
  c. eat at home instead of buying breakfast on the way to work every day and save $200 a month
  d. save the money instead of buying her asthma medication

14. Which is a judgment, not a fact?
  a. That production of *Hamlet* was first-rate; you'll never see it done better.
  b. That production of *Hamlet* was first-rate; it was cited as such in the *Daily News*.
  c. That production of *Hamlet* was first-rate; it won an award this year.
  d. That production of *Hamlet* was first-rate; 94% of audience members interviewed after the show agreed.

15. What is wrong with the following argument?

America—love it, or leave it!

  a. There is nothing wrong with the argument.
  b. It implies that if you leave the country on vacation, you do not love it.
  c. It does not tell you how to love it.
  d. It presents only two options, when in fact there are many more.

16. Which of these situations does NOT require problem solving?
  a. After you get your new computer home, you find there is no mouse in the box.
  b. When you get your pictures back from being developed, you realize they are someone else's.
  c. Everyone on your team wants to celebrate at the Burger Palace, but you just ate there last night.
  d. You've been assigned to finish a report for tomorrow morning, but it is your son's birthday, and you promised you would take him to the ball game tonight.

17. Which type of website most likely provides the most objective information about Abraham Lincoln?
  a. the home page of a history professor who wrote a book on Lincoln's presidency
  b. a Confederate group's site on famous assassinations, with the most pages devoted to Lincoln
  c. the site of a historical preservation group that archives Lincoln's correspondence
  d. the official site of the presidential library in Springfield, Illinois, devoted to telling the life story of the 16th president

18. Which is NOT a likely cause of this situation?

"I can't turn on the lamp in the family room!"

a. The lamp isn't plugged into an electrical outlet.
b. We just bought a new couch in a color that matches the lamp.
c. There's a power outage in the neighborhood.
d. The light bulb in the lamp has burned out.

19. What is wrong with the logic of the following statement?

"How can you believe his testimony? He is a convicted felon!"

a. The fact that the person testifying was convicted of a crime does not mean he is lying.
b. A convicted felon cannot testify in court.
c. The person speaking has a bias against criminals.
d. The person speaking obviously did not attend law school.

20. Evidence shows that people who live in the Antarctic score higher on happiness surveys than those who live in Florida. Which is the best conclusion that can be drawn from this data?
a. Floridians would be happier if they moved to the Antarctic.
b. People in colder climates are happier than those in warmer climates.
c. There are only happy people in the Antarctic.
d. Those in the Antarctic who scored high on a happiness survey probably like snow.

21. Which of the following is a sound argument?
a. Rain was predicted yesterday, so I took my umbrella to our outdoor rehearsal of *Romeo & Juliet*. It didn't rain. To make sure it doesn't rain during today's rehearsal, I'll take my umbrella with me.
b. You and Danny broke up the night you had dinner at Mangano's, so don't worry; you and Max won't break up as long as you never go to Mangano's!
c. My science teacher bases a lot of our grade on class participation. Last quarter, he said I needed to participate more. If I want a better grade this quarter, I need to take part in more class discussions.
d. Our washing machine is broken. The last time we had trouble with it, we hired a new repairman. He's probably the reason the machine broke!

Read the following paragraph and answer questions 22 and 23.

I always knew I wanted to be a marine biologist. When I was six, my parents took me to an aquarium, and I was hooked. But it was in college, when I got to work on an ocean research cruise, that I decided to specialize in oceanography. The trip was sponsored by the Plankton Investigative Service, and our goal was to collect as many different types of the microscopic plants and animals as we could, in order to see what, if any, impact the increased number of people fishing there had on the marine ecosystem. Our group was divided into two teams, each responsible for gathering a different type of plankton. Working with the phytoplankton, especially the blue-green algae, was fascinating. We measured the chlorophyll in the water to determine where, and in what quantity, the phytoplankton were. This worked well because the water was so clear, free of sediment and contaminants.

22. What is phytoplankton?
   a. another name for chlorophyll
   b. a microscopic plant
   c. a microscopic animal
   d. a type of fish

23. The goal of the study group was to investigate whether more people fishing in the area had
   a. a positive impact on the local economy.
   b. depleted the supply of fish.
   c. made more work for marine biologists.
   d. a negative impact on the health of the surrounding waters.

24. You want to sell your three-year-old car and buy a new one. Which website would probably give you the best information on how to sell a used car?
   a. Auto Trader: get the latest pricing and reviews for new and used cars; tips on detailing for a higher price
   b. Better Business Bureau: provides free consumer and business education; consult us before you get started in your new business!
   c. New Wheels: research every make and model of Detroit's latest offerings
   d. Car Buying Tips: everything you need to know before you shop for your new car

25. Which explanation is weakest?
   a. The steak was overcooked because I cooked it too long.
   b. Jose didn't drive his car today because it was in the shop for repairs.
   c. We don't belong to the country club anymore because we can't afford it.
   d. Gabrielle overslept because she stayed up very late last night.

26. Which of these problems is most severe?
   a. Your professor is sick and misses class on the morning you are supposed to take a big exam.
   b. You lose track of your schedule and forget to study for a big exam.
   c. You can't find one of the books you need to study for a big exam.
   d. The big exam is harder than you thought it would be and includes a section you did not study.

27. Which is the most important reason for evaluating information found on the Internet?
   a. Authors who publish on the Internet are typically less skilled than those who publish in print.
   b. Web writers are usually biased.
   c. Anyone can publish on the Internet; there is no guarantee that what you are reading is truthful or objective.
   d. Information found in print is almost always more accurate than that found on the Internet.

28. What is wrong with the following argument?

"We should not change our grading system to numbers instead of letters. The next thing you know, they will take away our names and refer to us by numbers, too!"

a. The conclusion is too extreme.
b. There is nothing wrong with the argument.
c. Students should not have a say in the type of grading system used in their schools.
d. It does not explain why they want to get rid of letter grades.

29. What is the real problem, as opposed to being an offshoot of that problem?
a. Your bank charges a $40 fee for overdrafts.
b. You wrote a check at the grocery store, but did not have the money to cover it.
c. Every month, you spend more money than you earn.
d. Last month, you paid $120 in overdraft charges to your bank.

30. Which is an example of hyperbole?
a. The deck of our boat was as slippery as melted butter!
b. This bag of groceries weighs a ton!
c. Onto each life some rain must fall.
d. Marco's lasagna is better than Mira's.

Pretest Answers

1. **a, c, d** (Lesson 3)

2. **c.** (Lesson 9)

3. **d.** (Lesson 14)

4. **c.** (Lesson 6)

5. **b.** (Lesson 15)

6. **c.** (Lesson 4)

7. **a.** (Lesson 11)

8. **d.** (Lesson 7)

9. **c.** (Lesson 3)

10. **b.** (Lesson 16)

11. **c.** (Lesson 17)

12. **c.** (Lesson 12)

13. **c.** (Lesson 5)

14. **a.** (Lesson 18)

15. **d.** (Lesson 13)

16. **c.** (Lesson 1)

17. **d.** (Lesson 8)

18. **b.** (Lesson 14)

19. **a.** (Lesson 16)

20. **d.** (Lesson 10)

21. **c.** (Lesson 15)

22. **b.** (Lesson 19)

23. **d.** (Lesson 19)

24. **a.** (Lesson 7)

25. **a.** (Lesson 18)

26. **b.** (Lesson 1)

27. **c.** (Lesson 8)

28. **a.** (Lesson 13)

29. **c.** (Lesson 2)

30. **b.** (Lesson 9)

LESSON

1 ▶ RECOGNIZING A PROBLEM

We are continually faced with a series of great opportunities brilliantly disguised as insoluble problems.

John W. Gardner, American politician, former Secretary of Health, Education, and Welfare (1912–2002)

LESSON SUMMARY

If you want to begin to think critically so you can solve problems, you first have to recognize that there is a problem and decide its importance or severity. This lesson focuses on how to do just that!

We all face problems every day. Some are simple, like running low on gas in your car, and take a short period of time to solve. Others are complex and demand more time and thought. For example, someone's boss might ask him or her to figure out why the company's latest sales pitch to the most important client failed, and come up with a new one.

Once you know you have a problem, you need to prioritize—does the problem demand immediate attention, or can it wait until you are finished working on something else? If there's more than one problem, you need to rank them in order of importance, tackling the most important first.

What Is a Problem?

A problem is defined as a question or situation that calls for a solution. That means when you are faced with a problem, you must take action and make decisions that can lead you to a resolution.

Problems that occur in the form of questions typically don't have one easy answer. Imagine you're asked, "Why are you voting for candidate X instead of candidate Y?" or "Why do you deserve a raise more than Tannie does?" You know the answer, but it's not always easy to put it into just a few words.

Situational problems require thinking analytically and making decisions about the best course of action. For example, Raquel learns that a coworker has been exaggerating the profits of the company for which she works—and he is doing it on orders from the company president. Should Raquel blow the whistle, jeopardizing her career? If so, to whom?

Road Block to Recognizing a Problem

One of the most common reasons for not recognizing a problem is a desire to avoid taking action or responsibility. People think that by not acknowledging the problem, they have no responsibility for solving it. This kind of thinking can cause someone to "not notice" there are only five checks left in his or her checkbook—if acknowledged, he or she would need to order more checks. Or, a worker looks the other way as faulty items come off a conveyor belt and are packed for distribution—if noticed, this should be reported to management. Then the worker might be asked to find out what went wrong.

If people don't acknowledge a problem, it could become larger and more complex, or more problems might be created. For example, if the person in the first situation doesn't notice a need for more checks and order them, he or she will run out of checks. Then, the person not only will be without checks when they're needed, but will have to go to the bank for temporary ones. And if a worker fails to report the faulty products, there could be lawsuits that might cause the company to cut staff, including the worker who first saw (but failed to recognize) the problem. Always remember, failing to recognize a problem usually creates more work—and more problems.

TIP

A wise man, Theodore Roosevelt, once said, "In any moment of decision the best thing you can do is the right thing, the next best thing is the wrong thing, and the worst thing you can do is nothing."

But Is It Really? Determining the Existence of a Problem

Some situations look like problems when, in fact, they're not. How can you tell? Ask yourself, "Is this just part of a process or does it actually call for a solution?" It's important to recognize when problem-solving skills are needed, and when they aren't. Here's an example:

George has spent two weeks training a new employee at the bank where he works. The new employee makes a couple of errors during her first day out of training. Should George ask his boss if he can spend more time with her? Or, should he find out what expectations the boss has for new employees? George discovers that the boss expects a few errors during a teller's first week on the job. So what George thought was a problem wasn't really a problem at all.

Types of Problems

Once you recognize that a problem exists, but before you begin to solve it, you have to determine the type of problem as it relates to a timeframe and your personal priorities. There are two criteria to use: **severity** and **importance**.

Severe Problems

Severe problems may be identified by the following characteristics:

- require immediate solutions
- may call for the involvement of others who have more expertise than you
- result in increasingly drastic consequences the longer they remain unsolved

For example, a break in your house's plumbing is a severe problem. Water will continue to leak, or perhaps gush out, until the break is fixed. The water can damage everything it comes in contact with, including hardwood floors, carpeting, furniture, and walls. Unless you are a plumber, you will need to call a professional to solve the problem immediately. Delays can result in a more difficult plumbing issue and also costly water damage repairs. You might even need to replace flooring or other items if the break is not fixed quickly.

Some minor problems can become severe if not solved immediately. For example, a campfire in the woods that is difficult to put out may take a great deal of time and effort to extinguish. But if it is not put out, it could start a major forest fire (severe problem).

Practice

Three problems arise at work simultaneously. In what order do you solve the following?

a. The printer in your office is down.
b. You need to finish writing a report to meet a 3:00 P.M. deadline.
c. Documents must be dropped off at the post office by 5:00 P.M.

Answer

The most sensible order is **a, b, c**. You can't print the report without the printer, so it must be fixed first, and if a repair person must be called, this task could take the most time of the three. Then, write the report. When you're finished, print the documents, or if necessary copy them on disk and take it to a printer off-site, and then take the printed material to the post office.

Practice

You invited friends over for pizza and a movie. Before they arrive, you preheat your oven to keep the pizzas warm and put the movie in the DVD player to fast forward through all of the coming attractions and advertisements. However, the DVD is damaged and will not play. As you head out to exchange the tape, you smell gas coming from the kitchen. What should you do?

_____

_____

_____

_____

_____

Answer

A natural gas leak is a severe problem and must be dealt with first. You should turn off the oven immediately, air out the room, and take great care not to light any matches. Then you should call the apartment superintendent to report the leak so he can check out the oven. The other problems aren't severe. You can call your friends to have them wait until the apartment is safely aired out, if the problem can be fixed quickly, and then choose another movie to watch. If the gas leak can't be fixed quickly, you can get out of the apartment and change the get-together until another day.

Practice

Which, if any, of these problems is severe?

a. Leo's baby has had the sniffles for several days, but she doesn't seem to have a fever.

b. Erin discovers a hole in her favorite shirt, which she wants to wear that day to start at her new job.

c. Will's rent is two months past due, and he doesn't have enough money to pay it.

d. The bus company is on strike, and Sandy has an important interview at 3:00 P.M.

Answer

Choice **c** is the most severe: Will might lose his home. If he calls the landlord immediately to explain and make arrangements, he could ward off eviction, or he could get a roommate to share expenses, using that person's first payment to help hold off the landlord. Choice **a** might become severe if a fever starts, but it is not necessary to take a baby to a doctor for every sneeze and sniffle. Choices **b** and **d** aren't severe: Erin can choose another shirt, and Sandy can find some other way to travel—walk, drive, ask a friend for a ride, or call a taxi.

TIP

Think of a problem as an opportunity to learn something and build your self-confidence. Every time you solve a problem, it gives you the confidence to face the next one.

Important Problems

Problems are considered important or unimportant in relation to one another, and according to personal priorities. That means you have to rank problems in terms of what's most important to you. By prioritizing, you don't deal with minor issues first, leaving more important ones until the last minute.

Practice

Rank these issues in order of importance to you, from most important (1) to least important (5).

the economy, global warming, universal healthcare, crime, education

1. _____
2. _____
3. _____
4. _____
5. _____

Answer

How you answered depends on your opinions and life circumstances. If the economy is weak, with unemployment and prices of everyday goods high, you might rank the economy most important. If someone in your family is ill and struggling to pay medical bills, healthcare may be your top concern. But if crime is on the rise in your area, or the education system is short-changing students, including you, you might rank one of those issues as most important.

Practice

You are planning a family vacation at a resort 800 miles from your home. Here are some of the details you will need to take care of:

- purchase plane tickets
- research restaurants in the area around the resort
- make reservations at the resort
- suspend delivery of mail and newspaper for duration of trip
- find a pet sitter for your cats

In what order should you complete these tasks?

1. _____
2. _____
3. _____
4. _____
5. _____

Which is most important?_____
Least important? _____

Answer

While there is room for various answers based on personal preference, here's the most common ranking by importance:

1. Make reservations at the resort—many places are crowded and you run the risk of having no place to stay unless you take care of this detail first.
2. Purchase plane tickets—you need to reach your destination, but if you can't get a flight, you might decide to rent a car.
3. Find a pet sitter for your cats—this shouldn't be difficult, but you can't go on vacation without finding help for the cats.
4. Suspend mail and newspaper delivery—a stuffed mailbox and piled-up newspapers are a sign to potential thieves that no one's home, but you can always call a neighbor after you get to the resort to ask for help if you forget to plan ahead.
5. Research restaurants—you'll have plenty of time after you get to the resort to read local publications and ask resort personnel. That kind of advice will probably be better than what you can research from home.

The Cost of Problem Solving

When you are on a budget, money is a factor in determining the importance of problems. If two or more problems require a payment to solve and you do not have the money available to take care of everything at once, you will need to determine what needs attention first and what can wait.

Practice

Perhaps you find that your car needs a new muffler the day before you were going to take your air conditioner in to be repaired. You do not have the money to do both right now. Make a list of the reasons each repair is necessary, and decide which should be done first.

Car Repair: _____

Air Conditioner Repair: _____

Conclusion: _____

Answer

Your lists will probably include many of the following:

Car Repair
- car will be too noisy without a muffler
- could be stopped by law enforcement and fined without muffler
- can't drive car without muffler
- need car to drive to work

Air Conditioner Repair
- AC running inefficiently—wasting electricity
- heat wave predicted for later in the week
- have trouble sleeping without AC
- live on fourth floor—too hot without AC

Conclusion: the car should be repaired first. While it may be uncomfortable without an air conditioner, you need your car to get to work, and that is your top priority.

In Short

When you recognize that you are faced with a problem, you also recognize the need for action on your part. But that action depends on the kind of problem you are facing. Is the problem severe? If there is more than one problem, which should be tackled first? Use your critical thinking skills to pinpoint any problem before you begin to anticipate a solution.

Skill Building Until Next Time

- The next time you need to make a To Do list, try ranking the items on your list. You might list them in order of what takes the most or least time. Or perhaps list them in order of when they have to be done. You might have your own order of importance in which to list items. For practice, try ordering them in each of the different methods previously listed.
- Test your skill of problem recognition when watching the evening news. After you hear a story, list three problems that will probably occur as a result.

2 ▶ DEFINING A PROBLEM

The significant problems we have cannot be solved at the same level of thinking with which we created them.

Albert Einstein, German-American scientist,
Nobel Prize winner (1879–1955)

LESSON SUMMARY

How do you know if something is a real problem or just looks like one? In this lesson, you'll find out how to tell the difference between those that are genuine and those that aren't. You'll also discover some common reasons people miss the real problems before them.

No matter what the problem, the only way to come up with an effective solution is to identify the actual problem that needs to be solved before you do anything else. If you don't, you could end up spending your time treating the symptom or consequence of your problem while the real problem remains waiting to be dealt with.

Have you ever spent time looking for a solution to something, only to discover that the real problem is still there, as big as ever? Here's an example. Pete worked for hours pulling up what he thought were weeds in his garden, only to discover a few days later that the very same stuff was growing back. What Pete failed to notice was that sunflower seeds from his birdfeeder spilled into the garden every time a bird landed there. Unless Pete moves the birdfeeder, or changes the kind of seeds he puts into the feeder, he'll continue to have a problem with sprouting sunflowers in his garden. The "weeds" were merely a consequence of the problem—the location and contents of Pete's birdfeeder.

Pete's problem represents a common error in problem solving. People often mistake a more obvious consequence of a problem for the *actual* problem. This can happen for different reasons. People may be busy, so whatever irritates them the most gets the most attention, or they may make assumptions about the nature of the problem and take action without determining if the assumptions are valid.

When someone "solves" a situation that's not an actual problem, there are two common results:

1. The "solution" is unsatisfactory because it fails to address the real problem.
2. Further decisions are needed to solve the real problem.

What Is the Real Problem?

Many times, it can be tricky to figure out exactly what the real problem is. Here's an example: Marta's teacher, Mr. Girard, returns her essay with a poor grade and tells her to rewrite it. With no other feedback, Marta doesn't know what's wrong with the essay, so how can she correct it effectively? In this case, it will take some work for Marta to define the problem. First, she needs to reread the essay carefully to see if she can figure out what's wrong with it. If the essay's problems are still not apparent to her, she needs to go to Mr. Girard and ask him to be more specific. Then, when he tells her exactly what's wrong with her work, she can redo it to meet his standards.

At other times, a problem may seem overwhelming in its size and complexity. People may avoid dealing with it because they think it will take too much time or energy to deal with such a large issue. However, a closer look might reveal that there may be only one real problem of manageable size, and a number of offshoots of that problem which will resolve themselves once you deal with the actual problem.

How do you go about defining the real problem? There are a few things to keep in mind.

- **Get the information you need**, even if you have to ask for it.
- **Do not be tricked into solving offshoots**, or other consequences, of your problem instead of the problem itself.
- **Do not be overwhelmed** when you are faced with what looks like, or what you have been told is, a giant problem.

Practice

What is the actual problem, and what is the perceived problem here?

The owner of an office building decides to add ten floors to increase the number of tenants. When construction is complete, the original tenants begin to complain about how slowly the elevators are running. The owner calls an elevator company, explains the situation, and asks them to install a faster elevator. He is told that there is no faster elevator, and that the problem is not the speed of the elevator, but

_____

_____

_____

_____

_____

Answer

The real problem is that the tenants must wait longer for the elevator because there are more of them using it and the elevator must travel to more floors than before. The tenants' perceived problem is the new slower speed of the elevator. In reality, the elevator is moving at exactly the same speed as before.

Practice

What is the real problem, and what are the offshoots of that problem?

a. There is a leak in the roof.

b. A heavy tree branch fell on the house during a storm.

c. A large, dead oak tree is located next to the house.

d. The bedroom floor has water damage.

Answer

The dead tree, choice **c**, is the real problem. If it is not removed, the homeowner can repair the floor, the roof, and remove the branch but the next time there's a storm, another branch could break off and he'd end up with the same problem.

Practice

What is the actual problem in this situation?

> While on vacation, Ryan withdrew money from his checking account using his debit card. The account balance went to $0, but the check he wrote for the water bill before he left came into the bank for payment. Although he has overdraft protection, the bank charged him a fee for insufficient funds, and returned the check to the water company, which is also charging a returned check fee.

Identify the real problem from the following choices:

a. He owes money to the bank and the water company.

b. The bank made a mistake by not covering the check.

c. Ryan's vacation cost more than he budgeted for.

d. Ryan does not have enough money in his checking account.

Answer

The real problem is choice **b**. The bank should have used the line of credit Ryan set up in advance as overdraft protection to cover the check. He needs to alert the bank of the error and have someone contact the phone company about the erroneously returned check.

TIP

Learn to recognize the difference between a true problem and its offshoots and you'll discover that what appears to be a daunting problem is actually quite doable.

Distinguishing between Problems and their Symptoms or Consequences

How can you be certain you are dealing with real problems rather than their symptoms or consequences? There are two things you can do whenever you believe you need to find a solution: avoid making assumptions, and think the situation through.

Avoid Making Assumptions

What is an assumption in terms of problem solving? It is an idea based on too little or not very good information. For example, the manager of a convenience store has an employee who is often late for her shift. The manager makes the assumption that the employee is lazy and does not take her job seriously. In fact, the employee has had car trouble and must use unreliable public transportation to get to work.

When you avoid making assumptions, you get all the information you need before deciding anything. With the right information, you can see the problem clearly rather than focusing on its consequences or mistaking them for the real problem. Then you can work toward a satisfactory solution. For instance, when the manager realizes that transportation is the real problem, she might be able to help the employee find another way to work rather than reprimand her for being lazy.

TIP

Accept the problem for what it is. When you stop resisting, you put more energy into finding solutions.

Practice

Write (A) for each assumption. If it is not an assumption, leave it blank.

____ 1. I've never made pizza from scratch before, but I think it should be simple to make.

____ 2. George said he's looking for a second job because he needs more money.

____ 3. The secondhand smoke in the air makes it hard for some people to breathe.

____ 4. The others on this art project aren't doing a good job because they don't want to work with me.

____ 5. Meg couldn't bake cookies for the party because her oven was broken.

Answers

1. (A) It's an assumption that making pizza from scratch is easy; it could be hard.

2. Not an assumption, George explained why he's taking a second job.

3. Not an assumption, smoke definitely can make breathing hard for some people.

4. (A) It's an assumption to think people don't do well because they don't want to work with someone; there could be other reasons, including a lack of talent or commitment!

5. Not an assumption, Meg couldn't bake without the oven.

Think It Through

To help you distinguish between problems and their symptoms or consequences, think it through. Ask yourself, "What is really happening?" Look at the problem carefully to see if there is a cause lurking underneath or if it is going to result in another problem or set of problems. Thinking it through allows you not only to define the issue(s) you face now, but can help you anticipate a problem or problems (see Lesson 7 for more information about predicting problems).

Practice

What problems might result from the following scenario?

The citizens of Colchester voted against three school budgets in elections held in April, May, and June. As a result, all school hiring and purchasing was put on hold. The school board then recommended cutting two teaching positions, which would save the town $92,000 in salary and benefits. At the election in July, the townspeople approved the new budget.

_____

_____

_____

_____

_____

Answer

Initially it may look like the town solved the problem, but in reality they've created some new problems. With the loss of two teachers, fewer classes will have to accommodate the same number of students. And since the budget was approved just weeks before school was to start, the remaining teachers might find it difficult to get needed supplies.

Defining a Problem within a Group

If it is sometimes difficult to distinguish between real and perceived problems on your own, the difficulty is much greater when you are told of a problem by someone else. For instance, your boss asks you to call a meeting for all paralegals to explain how to correct the problem of poor communication. "Why aren't Kyle's e-mails getting read by the attorneys on time?" he asks.

Often, pinpointing the real problem involves figuring out if the right question is being asked. The boss's question implies that he somehow wants the paralegals to change the way they send e-mails. But after checking things out, Kyle discovers that the lawyers just don't check their e-mails often enough. So the problem can't be solved by asking, "What can the paralegals do differently?" It can be solved by asking, "How can we get the attorneys to read their e-mails more frequently?"

When you are certain you are dealing with a real problem and you must solve it in or as a group, you must lead others to see that real problem. Some may be focused on the symptoms or consequences of it, while others may have made assumptions about the problem. In order to find a successful solution, everyone needs to clearly understand the problem.

Practice

Alexis's club chose her to head a committee to raise money for a local charity. The group hopes its fundraiser will help children in need. Which is the most important discussion topic at the first committee meeting?

a. Who will provide snacks for the next committee meeting?

b. Do we need to have weekly or bi-weekly committee meetings?

c. Who will write the thank-you notes to donors?

d. What kinds of fundraising activities can we do to raise the most money?

Answer

The best answer is choice **d**. It's up to Alexis, as head of the group, to steer attention to the real problem: how the group can raise money for the charity. By stating the problem, she opens the floor for brainstorming of ideas. The other topics may seem important, but are things that can be dealt with after the major discussion.

Roadblock to Defining a Problem

Often the biggest impediment to defining a problem is speed. When you are busy, especially on the job, you may be tempted to simply deal with superficial evidence, especially when it comes in the form of an aggravation or irritation. In such as case, you act quickly, rather than stop to look and see if the problem is merely the symptom of a larger or more serious issue.

However, what seems like a time saver (quickly resolving an aggravating situation) could actually cost you more time in the long run. If you have mistakenly identified the symptoms of a problem as the true problem, as stated earlier in this lesson, then your solution will be inadequate and the real problem will still be there.

In addition to wasting time by focusing on the false problem, you should keep in mind that there are many instances when doing the right thing is actually faster and simpler that dealing with the symptoms of a problem. For instance, in the elevator scenario described previously, the real problem is that the tenants do not like the effect the extra floors have on their elevator use. When the problem is defined this way, you eliminate expensive and complicated solutions such as where to buy faster elevators or how to construct additional elevator shafts.

TIP

Solving problems is mainly a skill of recognizing patterns and then using techniques you've seen before.

In Short

Effective problem solving begins with the identification of the real problem, as opposed to the perceived problem. Do not allow the size of the problem, your own assumptions, or a lack of information stand between you and an effective solution. Think the situation through, and do not be tempted to deal quickly with consequences or symptoms of your problem instead of the actual one.

Skill Building Until Next Time

Have you ever tried to follow a recipe, only to discover three steps into it that you're missing an ingredient or that the food will need to cool in the refrigerator overnight? Always read instructions thoroughly before you begin any process so you have all the information, and utensils, you need.

The next time you try a new recipe or set up equipment, like a DVD player or a new bookcase, spend at least ten minutes reading and reviewing the instructions first. Effective problem solving happens when you know exactly what you're facing.

3 ▶ FOCUSED OBSERVATION

In the field of observation, chance favors only the prepared mind.

Louis Pasteur, French scientist (1822–1895)

LESSON SUMMARY

It's important to be aware of what's going on around you. That way, you can spot problems that arise. This lesson is about increasing your awareness so you not only observe problems, but participate more skillfully in decision making and problem solving at home, work, and school.

To improve your critical thinking skills, you have to be more attuned to what's going on in your environment. If you consistently use focused, not casual, observation, you're more likely to notice when your input is needed. When you focus, you increase your awareness to what's going on and process the information more skillfully.

Increasing Awareness

There are three important things you can do to increase your awareness:

- Use your five senses.
- Get information from another person.
- Actively seek information.

While all three can work well, there are potential hazards with each. Knowing the hazards and ways to avoid them will help you use your powers of perception proficiently.

Observation

You are continuously using your senses to observe your environment. For instance, you *see* that the gas gauge is indicating that your tank is near empty; you *hear* your dog barking when he needs to be let out; you *feel* the heat coming off a grill before putting your food on it.

But just using your senses to note things isn't enough to help you determine that a problem exists. You need to put things into context by making an inference, or an educated guess, to help you make sense out of things. In other words, you ask yourself, "What does this mean?"

For example, you are waiting for envelopes that contain information about pay raises. When the envelopes are passed out, a coworker who opens his envelope and reads their contents looks depressed. You have made an observation, but what does it mean? You can infer from the depressed look of your coworker that his raise is probably much lower than expected.

Practice

What can you infer from the following scenario?

Christie comes into class and sits in her regular seat in the front row. The teacher walks in, writes his name on the chalkboard, picks up the attendance book, and calls out the students' names to see who is present. Then he points to Christie and says, "If anyone has any assigned homework from last night, please give it to this girl now."

_____

_____

_____

_____

_____

Answer

From the facts, you can infer that the teacher is a substitute teacher. Why? He wrote his name, probably because the students didn't know who he was. If he were the regular teacher, he'd probably have known Christie's name and not called her "this girl." And he's unsure if students had homework from the day before, probably assigned by their regular teacher.

TIP

Think of things you've personally seen and done, as well as things you're read or seen in movies and on TV, to help you *infer*, or "read between the lines."

Direct Method

Sometimes you don't actually observe a problem yourself; it's presented to you by someone else. For example, Lisa's boss tells her he suddenly has to go out of town, but he's already scheduled an important meeting for the next day with four other top-level executives. The boss expects Lisa to reschedule it. Or, Mark's professor announces that she's going to include questions on tomorrow's exam from a section she hasn't covered in class. Everything Lisa and Mark know about their problems, for which they need to find solutions, was told to them by someone else.

Road Block to Increased Awareness

A potential hazard of the direct method is that the person informing you of the problem may not see the situation clearly. What he or she thinks is the problem may not be the true issue. Thus, you need to pay careful attention and not automatically assume that the information you have received is accurate. Try to substantiate it by seeking even more information about the problem before taking any action.

Practice

Some of Leo's classmates complain to him that the teacher, Ms. Alixon, unfairly graded their papers. (Leo thinks that maybe his grade was a little too low as well.) Several students remark that Ms. Alixon is known for grading low. The classmates ask Leo to represent them and report the seemingly unfair grading to the school administration. Leo agrees and the administrators set up a meeting, with Ms. Alixon in attendance. She explains that the real problem is that some students didn't follow her instructions; she told them to put their papers on her desk, but they put them in her mailbox instead, so she received them a day late. School policy dictates that late papers automatically receive one letter grade lower than those turned in on time. What could, and should, Leo and his classmates have done before going to the administrators to avoid this embarrassing situation?

Gathering Information

Another way to increase your awareness is to actively seek information. This method is typically used after you have discovered that a problem may exist. In the previous scenario, it would have involved talking with another person (his teacher) to get more information. But you can also gather information from more than one individual, or source, like surveys and opinion polls.

Focusing Your Observations

You have already learned some of the best ways to increase your awareness. To improve problem solving and decision making skills, you will need to take this awareness to the next level by focusing. No matter which way you are informed, you will need to apply yourself to get the most out of the information you receive. You must:

- **concentrate.** Give it your undivided attention.
- **create a context.** Look at the situation as a whole, instead of zeroing in on a small part.
- **be thorough.** Your observations must be extensive and in-depth.

Concentrate

Situations occur around you all the time. Many of them require little or no attention on your part, such as your commute to work each day by bus. When you are a passenger, you can allow your mind to wander or even read or take a nap. The driving of the bus is taken care of for you. However, if you commute by car you must pay great attention, both to the road and to other drivers.

In instances that call for your awareness, you must pay careful attention. Concentrate on what you are observing or hearing. Sometimes the most critical piece of information is tossed out as inconsequential, an afterthought that you might miss if you are not fully aware. For example, your teacher explains an assignment at the end of class. He writes on the board the period of history you are to write about and suggests some sources of information. After many of your classmates have closed their notebooks and grabbed their backpacks, he mentions that your papers must be no longer than six pages. If you had not been paying attention to all of his instructions, you would have missed this critical piece of information.

Practice

Rank the following situations by how much concentration (awareness) they require. (5 = most, 1 = least)

a. ___ watching TV
b. ___ brushing your teeth
c. ___ giving an oral report in class or at a club meeting
d. ___ reading a bill from the phone company
e. ___ walking home alone late at night

Answers

You may rank these differently, depending on your personal situations, but here's one possible ranking.

5. **e**. Depending on where you live, walking at night may need all your attention so that you're always aware of people and sounds around you and are prepared in the event of a situation that might become dangerous, such as a mugging.

4. **c**. When giving an oral report, you need to concentrate on the words you're saying and the speed in which you're saying them, and may need to refer to your notes. You also need to be aware of audience reaction so if people applaud, you pause, and if they look bored, you can cut your remarks short!

3. **d**. When reading a bill, you need to concentrate on the charges to make sure you're not being charged for something you didn't buy/use, but you are still aware of people and sounds around you.

2. **a**. When watching TV, you give most of your attention to the show, and changing channels if you prefer something else, but you may talk to others or stop to answer the phone.

1. **b**. When brushing your teeth, you may be "on automatic." It's something you do every day and doesn't require concentration.

Create a Context

Focusing your observations also means bringing together many pieces to make a whole. In order to make sense of what you see or hear, you need to create a context for it—understand your observations in terms of their surroundings. Imagine someone tells you about a problem that he or she wants you to solve. The context in this case might be everything that person has said to you before. Perhaps he or she is constantly complaining about problems, many of which are not really worth your time. In that context, the new problem is probably also something you do not need to concern yourself with.

In contrast, imagine that you hear strange noises coming from under your car while you're driving down the highway. You suddenly remember that yesterday morning you saw a puddle of fluid on the garage floor under the car, and that you had some trouble starting the car in the supermarket parking lot that morning. You put the pieces together to create a context for the strange noises, leading you to take the car to a mechanic for a checkup.

> **TIP**
>
> Look for patterns. Is this problem like one you've had before? How did you solve that one?

Practice

You are asked to bring corn-on-the-cob to a friend's cookout. When you get to the store, you find that they have no corn. You try two other supermarkets, but they have no corn either. What pieces of information can help you create a context for this problem?

1. you heard a news story about a virus that attacks corn
2. your local supermarket is understaffed
3. you saw farmers spraying their corn crops
4. your friend does not like to cook

Answer

The most likely answers are **1** and **3**; the local corn crop might have been infested. An understaffed grocery store couldn't affect the corn supply, nor could your friend's dislike of cooking. How could you solve the problem? Take frozen corn-on-the-cob to the party!

Be Thorough

To best understand the situations you face, you need to look at them from many angles and take in as much information as you can. For example, you are attending a major league baseball game. Your seat is on the third base line. The opposing team's best hitter is right-handed, and the first time he was at bat, he hit the ball into the stands a couple of rows in front of you, where it barely missed another fan's head. With that observation in mind, what kind of attention will you pay to the game, especially when that hitter is at bat again? If you are thorough, you won't just watch the scoreboard or your team's outfielders. You will observe the batter hit the ball and watch to be sure you are not in harm's way (or that you are in the right place to catch a ball!).

TIP

Try putting yourself in someone else's shoes to view a problem from a new perspective. Ask yourself, "What would that person do?"

Practice

You are trying to decide which college to attend, and are visiting the three schools on your list of possibilities. You arrange an interview at each school with the admissions department. What things can you do to most thoroughly investigate the colleges? (circle all that apply)

   a. Write a list of questions for the interviews covering anything you did not learn about in the school's brochure and website.
   b. Ask to sit in on a class required in your chosen major.
   c. Tell the interviewer about your extracurricular activities.
   d. Eat lunch in the student dining hall.
   e. Pick up a recent copy of the school newspaper.

Answer

Only **c** is incorrect. All of the other ideas will help you to be thorough and get the most information from your visits.

In Short

When you increase your awareness, you make more sense out of your observations. Do that by using your senses, listening to what others say, and seeking more details. And when you are in the process of gathering information, concentrate, put it in context, and be thorough. You will not miss a thing if you pay careful attention—and you will become a better decision maker and problem solver in the process.

Skill Building Until Next Time

- Find a good spot for people watching, such as a coffee shop or outdoor café. Observe those around you, using your senses, with the goal of increasing your awareness. Is a couple about to have an argument? Is someone who is walking down the street without paying attention about to trip over a dog on a leash?

- The next time you are driving, make a mental list of the things you need to be aware of, and what might happen if you are not as observant as you should be. You might list an erratic driver, a child riding her bike, a utility company doing repair work from a parked truck, or an intersection regulated by four-way stop signs.

BRAINSTORMING WITH GRAPHIC ORGANIZERS

Make big plans; aim high in hope and work, remembering that a noble, logical diagram once recorded will not die.

Daniel Burnham, American architect and
city planner (1846–1912)

LESSON SUMMARY
Word webs, Venn diagrams, and concept maps are called graphic organizers because they do just that: organize ideas graphically. So they're really helpful when you're brainstorming your thoughts to find solutions to problems. In this lesson, you'll discover how to use them, and other graphic organizers, to your advantage.

Once you recognize and define a real problem, it's time to start looking for a viable, effective solution. That's why brainstorming is such an important critical-thinking skill in a problem/ solution situation. Brainstorming allows you to come up with as many ideas as possible, including way out-of-the-box suggestions, without making any judgments. You've probably done brainstorming before to generate ideas when assigned a group project in school or to plan a writing assignment. You probably made a list of ideas, or possible solutions, on paper. Then what?

While lists are good for recording information, they don't help you organize your thoughts very well. But graphic organizers do. They combine words and images so that you can see a lot of information at a glance. By visually arranging information, you can map your thoughts. That map can point you toward effective decisions and solutions.

Graphic organizers more effective than lists because they:

- are a meaningful display of complex information.
- help you see patterns and methods in your thinking.

- help you gather and compress information.
- keep you focused on the problem.
- show what you know and what you still need to find out.
- help you interpret your thoughts and ideas.

The types of graphic organizers covered in this lesson are:

- concept map: explores a simple topic or problem
- web: helps determine possible solutions for problems that have more than one cause or symptom
- Venn diagram: finds solutions by showing common ground between two or more causes or symptoms of a problem
- chart: compares and contrasts two or more elements
- problem/solution chart: outlines a problem, including its causes and effects, while producing possible solutions and outcomes to those solutions

Concept Map

Concept maps, also called target maps, should be used when you are exploring a topic that is not complex. To make one, draw a circle and add spokes radiating from it. Put your central idea or problem in the middle, and add possible solutions around it in any order. The following example visually arranges a simple decision and the factors that may be used in making that decision.

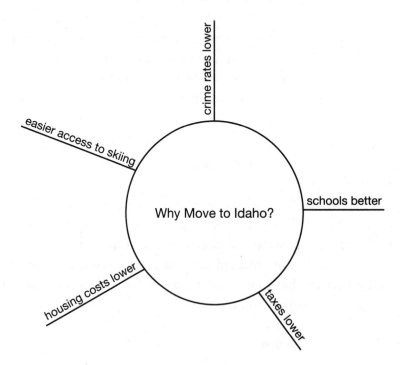

Practice

Imagine that you are considering joining a health club. Come up with at least five reasons why you should make the purchase. Use a concept map to organize your ideas.

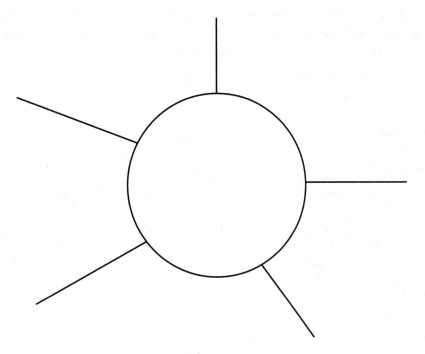

Answer

While there are many factors to consider, a possible map might look like:

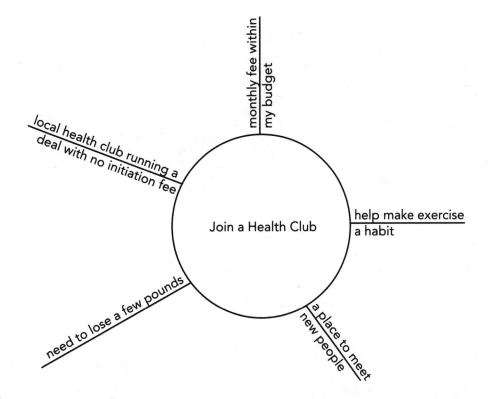

Webs

Webs are more structured and complex graphic organizers than concept maps. They're called webs because they look somewhat like a spider's web. These organizers help when you need to find possible solutions to a problem that has a number of causes. To create a web, write the problem in a circle. Next, write the causes in smaller, secondary circles and draw a line from each to the problem. Then, from each secondary circle, draw lines to other circles in which you list possible solutions. Here's an example:

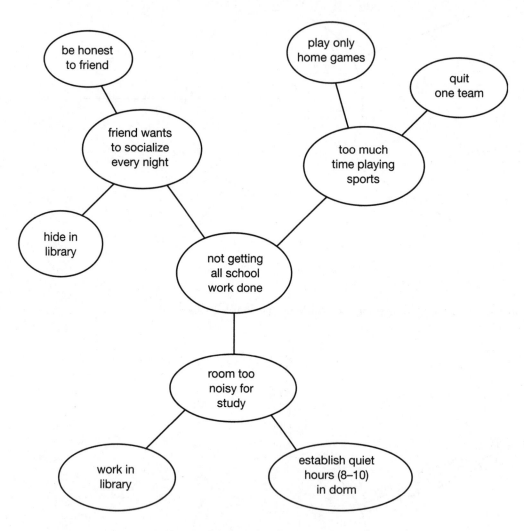

Practice

Create a web for the following problem: Sandy wants to deposit $50 per month of disposable income in an invest-ment account, but never seems to have the money. Causes of this problem are eating out at restaurants four times per week, not returning videos on time and paying late fees, and buying too many clothes. Brainstorm possible solutions for Sandy's problem using a web.

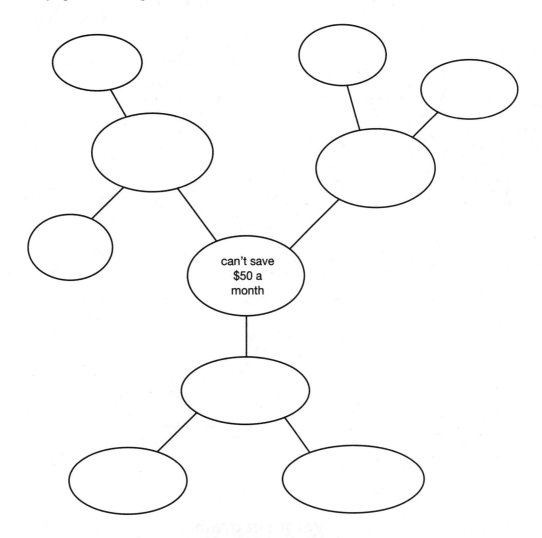

can't save
$50 a
month

TIP

Record all your ideas, no matter how outrageous or off-the-wall—focus on quantity, not quality. Let one idea give way to another idea.

Answer

Possible solutions:

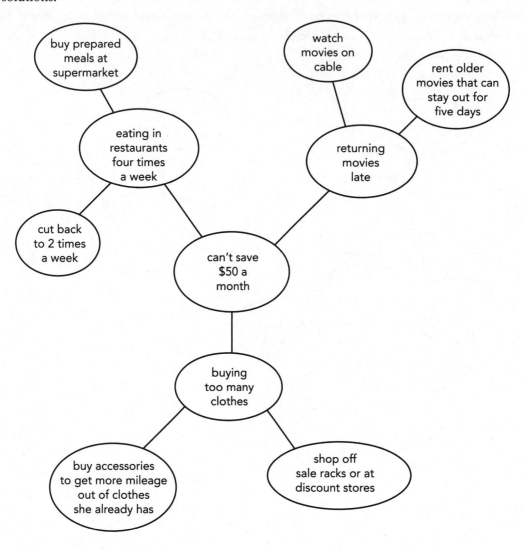

Venn Diagram

A Venn diagram shows the relationships among a group of objects that have something in common. Like a web, it is useful when you want to find solutions to a problem with two or three symptoms or elements. To create a Venn diagram:

- ask yourself, "What are the different symptoms of the problem?"
- write each element in a circle, and have each circle overlap (as shown on the following page)
- ask yourself, "What can I do differently to resolve each overlapping set of symptoms, or how can I use these elements together to arrive at a solution?" (circle A and circle B)

- repeat the previous step with circles B and C, and A and C
- fill in the overlapping areas with your responses

Example

You received $2,000 from the estate of a distant relative. You always wanted to travel to Europe, but you have also been trying to save money to renovate your bedroom. In addition, a local nursery is going out of business and the landscaping project you have only dreamed about could be yours for a 50% discount. To help determine what you should do with the money, create a Venn diagram showing the possible answers and ask yourself which is more important or deserving between each set of answers.

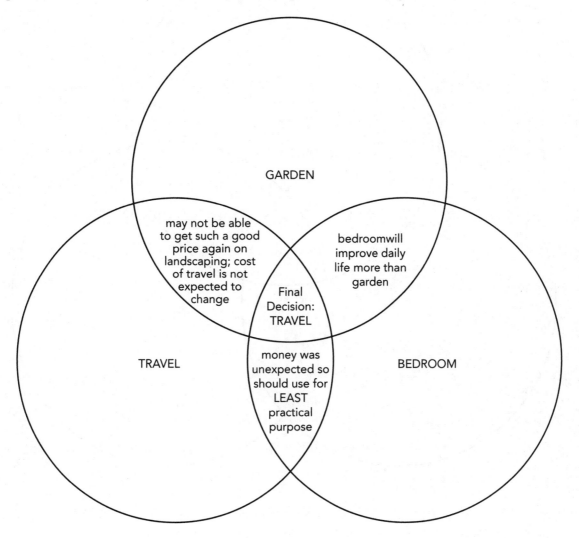

Practice

Michael is trying to figure out if he should ask for a raise. He's come up with three reasons for doing it: he needs more money for a growing family, he's taken on more work since a coworker left the company, and he hasn't had a raise in three years. Put each reason in one of the following circles, and then brainstorm how to translate Michael's reasons into a raise for him.

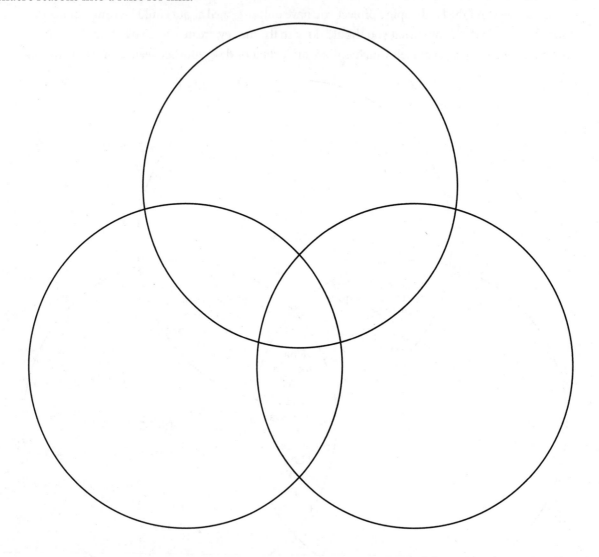

Answer

Possible answers for the overlapping sections are:

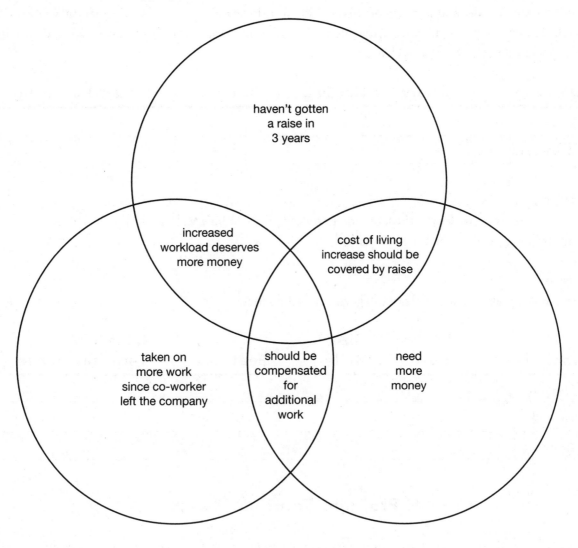

Chart

Charts are also great for comparing two or more things. They let you clearly see how each item is similar to and different from the others. To make a valuable chart, choose and write the things you want to compare, and then list two or more areas in which to compare them. You may need to do some research to accurately complete the chart, but it'll help keep you focused on your purpose as you do your research and work toward a conclusion.

Example

You are trying to decide whether to take a job offer in another state or stay where you are. The considerations are salary, housing, schools, and standard of living. While you already have the salary information, you will need to go to the library or Internet to find out the other facts you need to make your comparison. To guide you in your search, you create a chart that looks like this:

Decision	Salary	Housing	Schools	Standard of Living
Move to Chicago				
Stay in Atlanta				

Practice

Imagine you're trying to decide which brand of new cell phone to buy. Make a chart with categories to compare and contrast between several different brands.

Answer

One possible set of compare/contrast categories for cell phones:

Choices	Cost	Size/ Style	Features	Contract/ Termination Fee
Phone 1				
Phone 2				
Phone 3				

Problem/Solution Charts

The kinds of outlines that use Roman numerals, capital letters, Arabic numbers, and lower case letters are highly structured graphic organizers, so they don't work well for brainstorming. It's hard to come up with ideas quickly when you're trying to figure out where they fit into one of those number/letter outlines! Should this idea have a Roman numeral as a main idea or a capital letter as a supporting detail of that main idea? Or is it a secondary idea that supports the supporting idea? How time consuming and confusing!

Try a problem/solution chart instead. It's a more simply structured outline that can show the same information. Problem/solution charts are helpful because as you fill them out, you:

- clearly delineate the problem at hand, including causes and effects
- come up with solutions, and even possible outcomes of those solutions

Problem/Solution Outline Example

Problems (fill in as many as applicable)   Causes   Effects

Who: my family and me
What: should we buy a house or continue to rent a
    condominium?
Where: hometown
When: lease is up in two months
Why: possibly save money, build equity, improve quality of
    life
How: not applicable for problem
	rent is going
	up; neighbors
	are noisy
		If we buy: monthly payment
		would decrease, so have more
		money to save or invest; also
		would have more privacy and
		quiet. If we continue to rent:
		won't have moving expenses;
		will pay more in rent, so have
		less money to save or invest;
		will continue to have little pri-
		vacy and noisy neighbors

Possible Solutions

1. establish budget for home purchase, get pre-approved for mortgage, and go house hunting to see if we can find something in next two weeks within budget
2. remain in condo for another year while saving more money for a down payment

Possible Outcomes

1. find suitable house, secure mortgage, purchase house, move in
2. live with noisy neighbors for one more year, have bigger down payment and more time to look for house

---

TIP

The key to good outlining is to distinguish between the main idea and supporting details. A main idea is what something is mostly about; the details support, or tell more about, the main idea. In the previous scenario, the main idea is the dilemma of whether or not to buy a house. Everything else is a detail about that problem.

Practice

Your company has been selling its hammers to its distributors for $3 a piece. It costs $2.30 to manufacture each hammer. Your boss asks you for ways to decrease manufacturing costs in order to increase profits. Create a problem/solution outline to represent this scenario.

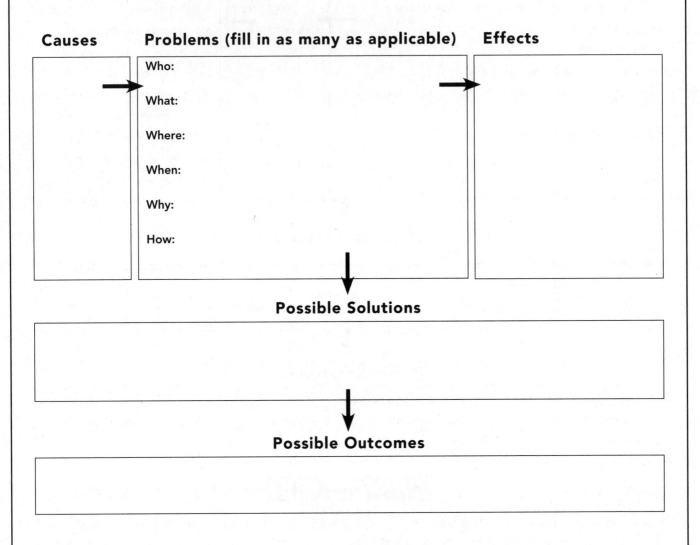

Answer
Problem/Solution Chart

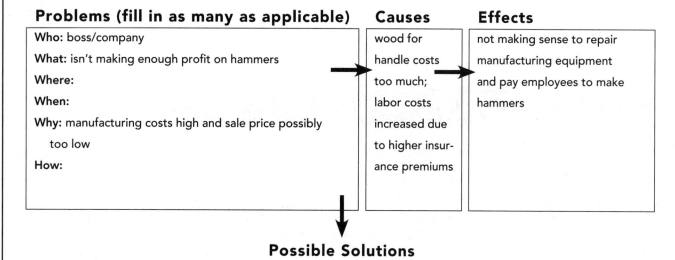

Problems (fill in as many as applicable)

Who: boss/company

What: isn't making enough profit on hammers

Where:

When:

Why: manufacturing costs high and sale price possibly
    too low

How:

Causes

wood for handle costs too much; labor costs increased due to higher insurance premiums

Effects

not making sense to repair manufacturing equipment and pay employees to make hammers

Possible Solutions

1. locate cheaper source of wood
2. get quotes to see if we can get less expensive insurance policy
3. raise price of hammer

Possible Outcomes

1. hammer would cost less to make and therefore profit would increase
2. if less expensive policy available, switch to it and save on labor costs, increasing profits
3. profits would increase, but retailers might choose to stock cheaper hammers instead

TIP

When you brainstorm, write for another five minutes even if you think you've run out of ideas. Only then should you begin to think through the ideas and narrow the list.

Roadblock to Brainstorming with Graphic Organizers

If you ever have trouble visualizing your problem or its solutions on graphic organizers, you may not have clearly defined your problem. It's virtually impossible to organize the information until you have a real understanding of what you're trying to achieve. Follow the advice in Lessons 1–3 to clarify the problem, and then try to create your graphic organizer again.

In Short

Graphic organizers are great tools for brainstorming. They create visual maps of your thinking, showing patterns and processes where you might not have expected them. Graphic organizers also keep you focused on your objectives, and can clearly point the way to effective solutions and smart decisions.

Skill Building Until Next Time

- Create a chart the next time you're deciding which restaurant to go to or where to spend your vacation. Compare criteria that's important to you, like ambience, service, food choices, beaches, child-friendly, shopping, and museums.
- Think of a problem you had to solve this past year. Make a web showing its causes and solutions, including not only the solution you actually used but many other possible ones.

5 ▶ SETTING GOALS

In the absence of clearly defined goals, we become strangely loyal to performing daily trivia until ultimately we become enslaved by it.

Robert Heinlein, American novelist,
science fiction writer (1907–1988)

LESSON SUMMARY

When you have a problem, you want to solve it, right? So you make a plan, or set a goal, to resolve the problem. The clearer you are about what you want to achieve and the steps you'll take to do so, the more likely you are to reach your goal. In this lesson, you'll discover how to do that.

A goal is a clear statement of something you want to accomplish or a problem you want to solve in the future. Goals may be personal, educational, or career oriented. For example: "I'm going to learn to play soccer this year," "I want to earn an A on my term paper," "I'm going to ask my boss for a raise in the next six months," or "I want to refinance my mortgage while rates are low." Whatever the goal, you need a step-by-step plan for reaching it. You also need to identify any obstacles in your way and things you might need, such as research or help from others.

TIP

Always set realistic goals over which you have as much control as possible. Don't set yourself up for failure because of reasons that are beyond your control.

Why Set Goals?

Lessons 1–4 covered defining, understanding, and focusing on problems, and brainstorming their possible solutions. Goal setting is the next important skill that will take you to those solutions. By setting a goal, you make things happen by focusing on exactly how to get from where you are to where you want to be.

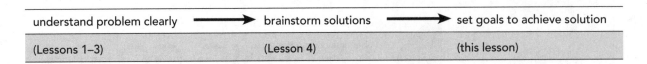

understand problem clearly	→	brainstorm solutions	→	set goals to achieve solution
(Lessons 1–3)		(Lesson 4)		(this lesson)

Five Qualities of a Sound Goal

Valuable goals are

- **in writing**—create a document of your goal
- **specific**—use as much detail as possible to explain what you want to accomplish
- **measurable**—describe your goal in terms that can be clearly evaluated
- **realistic**—don't set the goal too high or too low; you must be capable of reaching it with time and effort

- **deadline-oriented**—determine a completion date; the achievement of your goal must happen in a reasonable time, not "in a few weeks" or "some time in the future"

The following Goal-Setting Chart is a guideline. Depending on your goal, you may not need to fill out each section, or you may need to add a section or sections. Be flexible, but keep these five qualities in mind.

Here's an example of how a Goal-Setting Chart can help. Fran's grades aren't good and she knows she can do better. So first, she brainstorms possible solutions on a Problem/Solution Chart.

Goal-Setting Chart

Goal:

What is in my way:

How I will achieve my goal:

Step 1:

Step 2:

Step 3:

What I need to accomplish goal:

Timeline for accomplishing goal:

Daily:

Weekly:

When needed:

Monthly or long term:

What I will get from goal:

Problems (fill in as many as applicable)   Causes   Effects

Problems	Causes	Effects
grades are not good	too much time socializing; study skills weak →	parents upset, don't make honor roll, can't get into advanced level courses

Possible Solutions

limit time on phone and computer after school, pay better attention in class, buy and use workbook on improving study skills

To create a goal based on this problem, you will need to focus on the solutions you brainstormed, and create a plan to implement them effectively.

Goal-Setting Chart

Goal: to get no grade below a B next marking period (which ends March 14)

What is in my way: too much socializing, poor study skills

How I will achieve my goal:

Step 1: cut back on socializing: do not sit with friends during class; no phone calls or computer until home work is done

Step 2: improve study skills; buy workbook on study skills and complete one practice exercise every day; keep notebooks organized by cleaning them out every day after school; make a file folder at home for each class; do homework every day at desk; ask teacher(s) for help if I don't understand something

What I need to accomplish goal: study skills workbook, file folders

Timeline for accomplishing goal:

Daily: no socializing in class or after school until homework is done; study skills workbook, clean out notebooks; complete all homework assignments

Weekly: file assignments, tests, and quizzes

When needed: ask teacher for help; complete missing assignments

Long term: keep up plan for getting better grades

What I will get from goal: better education; feeling of accomplishment; name on honor roll; respect of parents and teachers

Practice

Think back to Lesson 4 and the situation about Sandy, who was trying to save $50 a month. You created a web to brainstorm possible solutions. Now, make the monthly investment a goal for Sandy, using any or all of the possible solutions you mentioned to complete the following goal chart.

Goal-Setting Chart

Goal:

What is in my way:

How I will achieve my goal:

    Step 1:

    Step 2:

    Step 3:

What I need to accomplish goal:

Timeline for accomplishing goal:

    Daily:

    Weekly:

    When needed:

    Monthly or long term:

What I will get from goal:

Answer

Using the brainstormed solutions from Lesson 4, the goal chart looks like this:

Goal-Setting Chart

Goal: to save $50 a month

What is in my way: spending too much so she does not have the money to invest (habits she needs to break)

How I will achieve my goal:

Step 1: limit restaurant meals to two times a week; buy takeout from supermarket other nights; buy cookbook and pick out one recipe a week to try

Step 2: rent one movie a week, put in briefcase when done watching it to return it on way to work

Step 3: limit clothing purchases to $100 a month; watch ads for sales and shop them

What I need to accomplish goal: willpower to change habits!

Timeline for accomplishing goal:

Daily: read newspaper for ads for clothing sales; shop for and/or eat dinner according to weekly plan

Weekly: rent one movie and return it the next day; make a plan for each night's dinner (restaurant, take-out, cooking)

When needed: shop for clothes on sale

Monthly or long term: set up investment account, and have $50 automatically withdrawn for bank account each month

What I will get from goal: money for long-term goals and/or emergencies

What Becomes a Goal?

When you are brainstorming, you come up with various possible solutions to a problem. But which one is worth pursuing? Goal setting is about choosing the best solution and creating a plan to make it happen. To do this, you need to clearly define your goal. What is it, exactly, that you wish for an outcome? Since every possible solution is different (by varying degrees) it can lead to different outcomes. Evaluate the ideas you came up with during brainstorming based on the specific criteria you set for your goal.

Example

You work for a company that manufactures running shoes. Compared to figures from a year ago, profits and sales are slumping. You are asked to come up with a solution that will increase both. While brainstorming, you come up with three possible solutions:

a. start a major marketing campaign
b. limit the availability of the product/service to increase demand
c. lower costs so that profit margins are increased

Let's look at these possible solutions and their probable outcomes. A large marketing campaign would most likely increase sales. Limiting the availability to increase demand would eventually lead to higher prices and greater profits, with a possible increase in sales. But lowering costs would most likely result in increasing sales and is a better way to increase both sales and profit. Therefore, it makes sense to choose solution **c**.

Practice

Charlene's bathroom needs a major repair because of a plumbing leak under the bathtub. She decides it's a good time to renovate the whole room since everything's outdated: the toilet tank is cracked, the faucets leak, the floor and wall tiles are an unappealing avocado green, and the tub will have to be destroyed in order to fix the leak. Charlene has worked out a budget by pricing new tiles, tub, vanity, sink, and toilet, and getting a quote from a contractor to install them. The problem is, she doesn't have $2,500 to pay for the renovation right now. After some brainstorming, she comes up with three possible solutions:

1. charge everything on a credit card
2. take out a home equity loan
3. have just the plumbing repair done now, which costs $700, and wait to do the rest of the job later

How should she proceed?

_____

_____

_____

_____

_____

Answer

There are several possibilities, depending on how you define Charlene's goal and evaluate the possible solutions. Her goal is to redo the bathroom because it's outdated and needs repairs. It seems like a good time because some tile and the tub will have to be torn out to fix the leaky pipe anyway. Charlene might charge everything on a credit card, but she first needs to know the interest rate, how much she'd have to pay each month, and how long it would take to pay off the card. Solution 2 might be a better choice, if the bank's interest rate is lower than the credit card rate, and she might be able to deduct the interest from her income tax. With Solution 3, she doesn't borrow any money or pay interest, but she'll still have to patch up areas temporarily where tile is removed, and some problems remain. So either solution 1 or 2, if not too costly, make sense since the plumbers will already be at the house.

TIP

Sometimes, despite all your planning, you may fail to reach your goal. Realize that it's just temporary, take it as a learning experience, and redirect your resources toward a new goal.

Roadblock to Setting Goals

An important thing to remember is not to set a goal that's too big or would take too long to accomplish. People often grow tired of their plans before they're completed. When you set a goal, can you picture yourself following the timeline to its conclusion? If not, break down the original goal into smaller, more manageable ones. Here's an example: Lennie sets a goal to ask for a raise in six months, so he made this goal-setting chart.

Goal-Setting Chart

Goal: I will ask for a raise in six months.

What is in my way: my job performance evaluation last month rated me "average"

How I will achieve my goal:

    Step 1: I will work longer hours and get more done at work

    Step 2: I will do become more knowledgeable about my company and figure out ways to use my skills to my and my company's advantage

What I need to accomplish goal: time, knowledge

Timeline for accomplishing goal:

    Daily: be the first one into work and the last one out at night

    Weekly: write a memo to my boss about what I have accomplished; check news for any stories about my company; read all material published by my company, including prospectus and other stock holders' information

    When needed: meet with my boss to tell her about special accomplishments

    Monthly or long term: check to see if I can help other employees with their projects

What I will get from goal: better evaluation, chance to get higher salary

In terms of objectives and timelines, Lennie is giving himself six months to improve his job performance and learn more about the company. But he expects to do everything at the same time for the next 26 weeks, which might be difficult. He would have a better chance of success if he set smaller goals one month at a time. For example, the first month he might concentrate on coming in early and leaving late to improve his image with his boss. Then, the second month, he might just work hard during normal business hours and read about the company at home on weekends. The third month, he could check out news about the company once a week while brainstorming ways to help other employees. By breaking down the large goal, he's more likely to reach it in six months.

Practice

Now set a short-term goal for yourself. Choose something relatively simple to do for 30 days, like reading a book or magazine for at least 15 minutes a day, cleaning out a closet and keeping it that way, adding at least one new word to your vocabulary every day, keeping a journal, trying new recipes, or exercising for 20 minutes a day. How should you proceed?

_____

_____

_____

_____

_____

Answer

Your answer depends on your goal. Here's one person's plan to meet one of the goals previously listed.

Goal: to exercise at least 20 minutes a day
- Do bending and stretching exercises when I wake up, before I take a shower.
- Do stretching exercises while watching TV or during commercials.
- Walk to the train station instead of getting a ride by car.
- Do a few bending/stretching exercises before getting into bed at night.

TIP

Success is a choice. You have to decide what you want and how you plan to reach your goal. No one else can or should do it for you.

In Short

Setting goals is an important part of problem solving, but always remember to set goals you can reasonably achieve. Use a goal-setting chart to create a map that can show you the way from the problem to the solution. The chart forces you to break down your goal into manageable steps, set a deadline, and spell out exactly what you'll do, and when. That exercise can help to move from where you are—facing a problem—to where you want to be—problem solved!

Skill Building Until Next Time

- Choose a short-term goal for yourself, such as a household repair. Using the list of five qualities of a valuable goal (see page 44), determine how you will get the repair accomplished. Set a deadline, be specific about what exactly you need to do, and write it all down as a visual reminder of what you will accomplish.
- Choose a longer-term goal, something that should take a few weeks or months to achieve. Make a goal-setting chart, breaking down the goal if necessary, and include every step you must take, and when. Follow your map and check off each task as you complete it on the way to achieving your goal.

LESSON

6 ▶ TROUBLESHOOTING

What we anticipate seldom occurs; what we least expected generally happens.

Benjamin Disraeli, British statesman and author (1804–1881)

LESSON SUMMARY
Sometimes things can go wrong as you follow your plan for reaching a goal or solving a problem. Small, or even large, stumbling blocks may appear and try to stall your forward progress. This lesson is about anticipating and dealing with any pesky obstacles that get in your way.

Troubleshooting involves thinking ahead, spotting problems even before they surface, or preparing to take care of them if they do. You anticipate what might go wrong and keep it from happening or, if something does pop up, keep it from growing into a major problem by resolving it while it's a manageable size. By doing so, you deal with any setbacks that might block the path to your goal. You have to learn to handle everything from small annoyances to major obstructions in order to get where you want to be. So troubleshooting is kind of like building bridges over troubled waters!

Identifying Problems That Interfere with Goals

After you set a goal and begin working toward it, you will inevitably be faced with a roadblock or two. You learned in Lesson 1 that you can't solve problems without first recognizing and accepting them, and that holds true for troubleshooting problems that interfere with your goals. Some of these problems are foreseeable; that is, you can anticipate them before you even begin to work toward your goal. Others are unexpected and must be dealt with as they arise.

Identifying foreseeable problems takes work. You have to honestly assess your goal and think critically about what might need to be overcome so you can achieve it. You saw an example of this in Lesson 5 when Fran set a goal to get better grades. She noted that her habits of "too much socializing" and "poor study skills" stood in her way. So, even before she began to work toward getting better grades, she knew what she had to overcome in order to be successful. Both obstacles were not simple for her to overcome because they required breaking troublesome habits and acquiring new skills.

Strange as it may seem, unexpected problems are usually easier to spot, and often easier to solve. For example, you're doing research and need a particular book from your local library. When you go to get it, you discover all copies have been checked out. Or you run into an unforeseeable technology problem, such as a computer crash or a printer breakdown as you're trying to finish a report for a deadline. All these problems are relatively easy to solve. In the first case, you can ask the librarian to check other libraries for the book, or even pick one up in a bookstore, if the price is reasonable. For the technology problems, you could find temporary solutions like working from a backup disk on someone else's equipment.

Unexpected problems, by their nature, can't be planned for. You must simply figure out the best way to solve them quickly and thoroughly, and then get back on your path. The rest of this lesson focuses on troubleshooting forseeable problems.

Practice

List at least two of each kind of problem that could arise in the following scenario. Note that while this example involves theatrical events, similar problems can occur anytime you have more than one thing to do and your schedule is tight.

At 10:30, Nan has a rehearsal of the play she wrote and is directing. She has to block the actors' movements in the second act as well as give them notes about their performances. Nan is also an actor herself, and has an audition scheduled across town for 12:30, where she's expected to perform two monologues and one song.

Foreseeable Problems:

_____

_____

_____

Unexpected Problems:

_____

_____

_____

Answers

Your answers might include:

Foreseeable Problems: Nan needs to prepare for both events, which could take more time than originally planned; working out the blocking and going over notes she gave the actors at the last rehearsal, as well as printing her updated resume and headshot and preparing the monologues and song for the audition. She may also need to contact the assistant director or several actors the night before and need to put off other tasks, like grocery shopping or laundry.

Unexpected Problems: the theater manager might be late and, without a key, Nan and her cast can't get in to rehearse, or one or more actors may not show up. Nan might have trouble getting to the audition on time because of traffic, late buses, or unavailability of taxis, and lose her chance to audition. Or, if she makes it to the audition on time, she might be asked to do a cold reading instead of the monologues, and be given just two minutes to look over the script. Or, the person who is auditioning the actors might be called away.

Troubleshooting Problems That Interfere with Goals

Troubleshooting foreseeable and potential problems can be difficult. It requires critical thinking skills to examine the path to your goal, and imagine or note all of the things that might go wrong as you work toward achieving it. For example, Dylan had minor outpatient surgery and received a bill for $8,500. He can submit it to his insurance company, which will cover 80% of the cost. However, the company has rules for filing claims, including that they be submitted no later than 30 days after treatment. If he waits two months before trying to get reimbursed, he will lose $6,880.

Let's look at Dylan's problem in terms of troubleshooting. He has a very expensive bill to pay and can solve that problem by filing an insurance claim because it's a covered expense. How could he determine the potential problems that might prevent him from being reimbursed $6,800? The best way is to read over the terms of his insurance policy. Does the company require preapproval before he goes to the hospital? Does the hospital bill the insurance company directly or does he have to file the claim? Is there a time limit for filing a claim? Once he understands exactly what's expected of him, his doctor, and the hospital, he can follow the terms of the policy to get the money. The potential problems are defined in this case in the policy terms for reimbursement. If Dylan doesn't follow all of them, the insurance company is not obligated to pay 80% of the bill.

Practice

Samantha agrees to take her friend's one-year-old son for an afternoon while he attends a business meeting. She didn't know much about children, other than having once been one herself. How can she troubleshoot the problems that she might encounter? Circle all answers that apply.

   a. Ask another friend with a baby to teach her how to change a diaper.

   b. Rent some videos a one-year-old boy might like.

   c. Read some child-rearing books.

   d. Do some comparison shopping for size 12-month clothes.

Answer

All except choice **d** are examples of troubleshooting. Samantha won't be expected to provide clothes for her friend's child, but she'll need to change his diaper and entertain him, and books, if she has time to read them, could give her some insight into what to expect from the average one-year-old and how to handle his needs.

TIP

As an old proverb says, "Forewarned is forearmed." Another says, "An ounce of prevention is worth a pound of cure." Wishing a problem hadn't happened does no good, but if you learn from the experience, you can try to head it off in the future if it comes up again.

Prevention Versus Cure

Another kind of troubleshooting involves looking for patterns and trends. If you're frequently faced with the same kind of problem, your best defense is to figure out what causes it and what you need to change so it doesn't happen again. You may need to change your own habits, but by doing so, you are preventing the problem rather than always trying to solve it!

Here's an example: Ned's boss meets with her supervisor every Friday morning to give an update of the department's progress. Ned starts to notice a trend. At 4:00 P.M. every Thursday, his boss begins to become irritable. And for the past few weeks, she's asked Ned to summarize what he and his colleagues have accomplished during the week. She always needs the summary in one hour, no matter what other urgent business Ned has to attend to. Some weeks, he's had to stop important work to write the summary, making his coworkers late with materials that needed his input. There are several ways Ned might prevent another such Thursday afternoon problem, rather than simply dealing with it the same way week after week. First, he should ask his boss if the summary will be his responsibility every week. If it will be, Ned could troubleshoot to prevent it from becoming a crisis by:

- asking his boss to alert the others in the department that every Thursday he'll be busy from 4:00–5:00 P.M., so everyone is clear about what he's doing.
- clearing his schedule on Thursday afternoons, or even begin work on the summary on Thursday morning or even earlier in the week.
- asking each coworker to give him a list on Thursday morning of all work done since the previous Thursday and any problems that arose, so he can easily compile the summary.

Following is a diagram you might want to use to explore possible troubleshooting methods. It can work for preventative troubleshooting or for anticipated problems that will occur whether you are prepared for them or not.

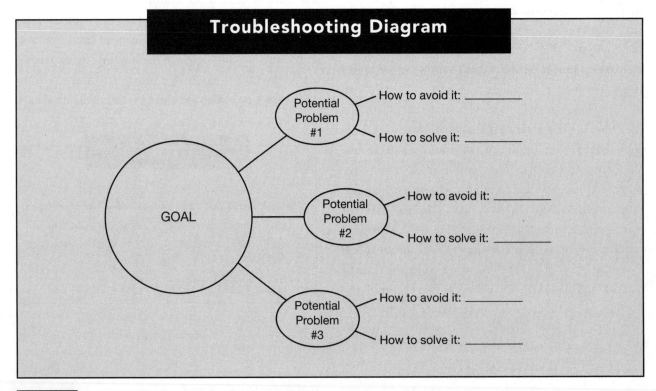

Troubleshooting Diagram

GOAL

Potential Problem #1 — How to avoid it: _____ / How to solve it: _____

Potential Problem #2 — How to avoid it: _____ / How to solve it: _____

Potential Problem #3 — How to avoid it: _____ / How to solve it: _____

Here is a diagram that shows what might happen if someone's goal was to graduate one semester early.

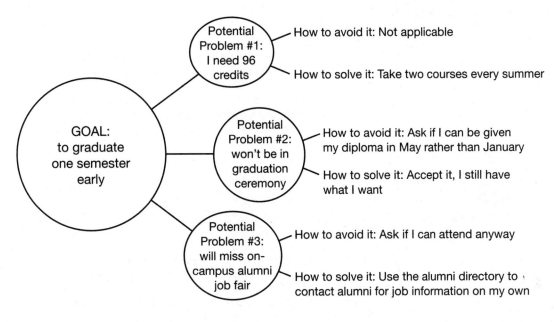

Practice

Image you are asked by your boss to order the food for your annual company picnic. She anticipates that 70 coworkers will attend. Last year, 65 people were at the picnic and they ate 50 hamburgers and 40 hot dogs. You know there will be a problem if you order too much or too little food. How can you troubleshoot these problems?

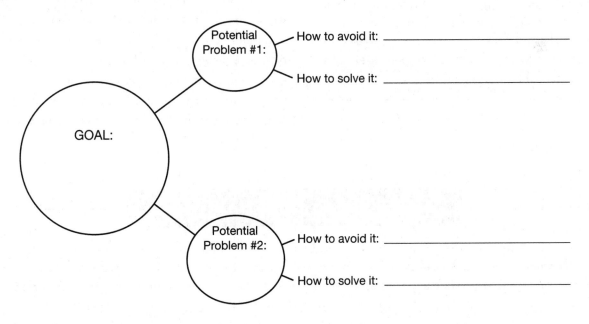

Answer

Answers will vary, but yours might include:

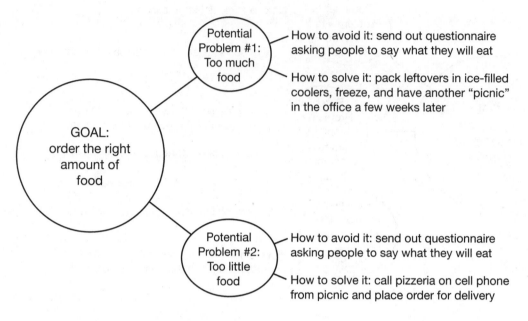

GOAL:
order the right
amount of
food

Potential
Problem #1:
Too much
food

How to avoid it: send out questionnaire
asking people to say what they will eat

How to solve it: pack leftovers in ice-filled
coolers, freeze, and have another "picnic"
in the office a few weeks later

Potential
Problem #2:
Too little
food

How to avoid it: send out questionnaire
asking people to say what they will eat

How to solve it: call pizzeria on cell phone
from picnic and place order for delivery

TIP

Keep a journal. When you do have a problem, write a complete, accurate description of what caused it and note the root cause. Make a damage control plan to prevent future repetitions of that problem.

In Short

Troubleshooting begins with identifying problems that will or may get in the way of you achieving your goals. You might know about them ahead of time, and even be able to prevent them, or keep minor problems from becoming major. Or, you may encounter them as they arise without warning. Either way, knowing how to find solutions and move forward will ensure that you reach your destination.

Skill Building Until Next Time

- Practice troubleshooting someone else's problems. When a friend tells you about his or her current dilemma, think about how the person might have prevented it or how he or she can solve it.
- Practice troubleshooting a global issue. Read a few articles on an issue of international importance, such as the crisis in the Middle East or global warming. Make a troubleshooting diagram to work through possible ways to avoid or resolve the problems that may or will result from this issue.

LESSON

7

FINDING RESOURCES

The greatest achievement of the human spirit is to live up to one's opportunities and make the most of one's resources.

Luc de Clapiers, French writer and moralist (1715–1747)

LESSON SUMMARY

Sometimes when you have to make an important decision, you don't have all the facts you need to help you make the best choice. Other times, especially at work or school, you may be asked to produce evidence to justify a decision you've made. In this lesson, you'll discover the best ways to find the information you need to make and justify decisions and solutions to problems.

Many decisions and solutions don't require a lot of work. After all, you don't need to gather much information to decide when to study for an exam or whether to bake a pie or a cake. You already know the facts, so you simply use them to make a wise decision. But what if you don't know which facts to base a decision on? What if there are things you aren't familiar with that really need to be considered? That's where thinking critically comes into play. You do whatever you can to find accurate information about the missing details, knowing that the quality of a decision is only as good as the information used to make it.

Let's look at three resources that can supply information to help you make decisions: the Internet, the library, and human sources. We'll explore each, when to use it, how to get the most out of it, and its possible shortcomings.

Internet Resources

Research on the Internet doesn't have to be confusing, even though you can literally access billions of websites. You just need to know what you're looking for and the best way to find it. There are three basic investigative methods. The first is to use a search engine, like *www. google.com*, *www.ask.com*, or *www.bing.com*, where you enter a topic, or words that relate to the topic, and are provided links to sites with information about that topic. But search engines don't always distinguish between useful and not-so-useful sites. They simply list everything, sometimes thousands of links that seems to meet your search criteria.

Another way to search the Internet is by using subject directories. The great advantage of this method is that the sites the directories list have been chosen by qualified people. Websites deemed to be of poor quality are less likely to make the directory. Some directories even hire experts in various fields to write guides to their chosen subjects and also to provide links to related sites. Recommended subject directories include:

- About.com (**www.about.com**): thousands of subjects with links to a million websites
- Academic Info (**www.academicinfo.net**): consistently maintained to add free educational resources (for late high school level and above) while weeding out outdated ones
- Librarians' Internet Index (**www.ipl.org**): over 20,000 Internet resources selected as "the best" by librarians
- Infomine (**http://infomine.ucr.edu**): aimed at university-level instructors and students, contains 110,000 Internet resources selected by university librarians

The third way to find what you are looking for on the Internet is to search directly on a site at which you believe the information may be found. Here is a short list of such sites.

Encyclopedias

Encyclopedia.com: a free site that aggregates content from numerous reference works including Columbia Encyclopedia and World Encyclopedia

Britannica.com: the first few paragraphs of each article are free, so if you need very basic facts, chances are you will get them; for an annual fee you can have total access to the site

Education.yahoo.com/reference: search the American Heritage Dictionary, Gray's Anatomy, the U.S. Government's World Factbook, and others

Dictionaries

Dictionary.com: searches a dozen dictionaries at one time

M-W.com: Merriam-Webster's Collegiate Dictionary searched free; access to the unabridged edition is available for an annual fee

Other Fact-Checking Sites

www.bartleby.com/reference: search for thousands of free online classics of literature and nonfiction, and reference materials like Bartlett's Quotations, Oxford Shakespeare, Gray's Anatomy, and World Factbook

www.bibliomania.com: search for author biographies, as well as through full texts of fiction, drama, and poetry

www.findarticles.com: search back issues of over 300 magazines and journals covering a wide variety of subjects

www.nilesonline.com/data: links to find statistics and other facts about government, crime, health, politics, and more

www.refdesk.com: find maps, calculators, currency converters, newspapers (from local United States to international), as well as dictionaries and encyclopedias

www.martindalecenter.com: check facts on everything from world poetry to organic chemistry, patents to computer viruses

Practice

Which of the following statements is NOT true?

a. Some research sites on the Internet make you pay for full access to information.

b. Search engines direct you to many links, but not necessarily the best sites to answer your research questions.

c. Search engines are not the only way to look for information on the Internet.

d. The only place you can research statistics is in a library.

Answer

The correct answer is choice **d** because you can find statistics at many sites on the Internet and can get them in other ways from other places, including calling or writing to a government or business association office or reading about them in daily newspapers.

Roadblock to Good Resources

What is the most common obstacle to finding factual, pertinent information? It is the proliferation of poorly researched, or even knowingly false, data. Primarily found on the Internet, fiction posing as facts, or simply slipshod work, can look like the real thing because legitimate websites with accurate content reside side-by-side with poor quality sites. It can be difficult to tell the difference.

The best way to avoid getting poor information is to be suspicious. Do not take any information you find on the Internet as truth until you can substantiate it with duplicate information on at least three other sites. Read the tips in Lesson 8 for more about evaluating the quality and content of websites.

> **TIP**
>
> Compare the ideas and arguments of a person with others in the same profession. The more his or her views differ from the majority on the subject, the more critical you should be of the ideas.

Practice

You are building a house and need to decide how to heat it. The contractor can put in a natural gas, propane, or electric furnace. You want to choose the option that is the least expensive to operate. A search on the Internet yields five results. Which website(s) will most likely have the information you need to make a decision?

1. the Environmental Protection Agency's site

2. site of the American Society of Heating, Refrigerating, and Air-Conditioning Engineers

3. an educational site about the use of wood in home heating units

4. corporate site for a retailer of electric powered home heating units

5. Kansas State University's Engineering Extension website

Answer

Numbers 2 and 5 will probably contain the most accurate, pertinent information. The EPA site considers environmental factors, such as pollution, which may result from certain types of home heating. The forestry site is not relevant to your decision. A retailer of furnaces is in business to make a sale, not necessarily to give you accurate information about how they compare to a competitor's product.

The Library—Print Resources

Although it might sometimes seem otherwise, everything of interest that has ever been written is not on the Internet, nor can it be searched for on the Internet. There are still five important reasons to do research at the library.

1. **Librarians.** These trained professionals know how to find what you are looking for, whether in the stacks or online.
2. **Non-searchable print.** Millions of books and other print materials have not made it to the web. In addition, the human power to key in or scan every old, deteriorating text, such as back issues of journals, magazines, and newspapers, does not exist. But they may be found in libraries, either in print or on microfilm or microfiche.
3. **Reliability of information.** Not all information on the Internet is accurate. Anyone can "publish" online, and it is not always easy to distinguish between reliable and unreliable websites. Many sites containing bogus information appear professional and well-written (see Lesson 8 for information on how to evaluate a website). Published books and periodicals, on the other hand, have been through many layers of safety nets before they reach the shelves of a library. They are typically written, edited, proofread, fact-checked, published, and then selected by a librarian for purchase.
4. **Finding anything that is not historical or current.** The Internet is a great resource for information that is either very old or very new. For instance, you can find the Magna Carta, and current state and federal statutes, but legal research on anything in the early to mid-20th century is difficult to nearly impossible to find on the Internet.

5. **Price.** The use of a library, including all of its electronic services, is free. Some of the research resources on the Internet are not. There are sites that give away some information, but charge for full access to their site. Others will not let you in at all unless you are a subscriber. Some Internet resources charge prohibitively high subscription prices. Libraries often pay these prices and provide full access.

Practice

List five types of information you are more likely to find in a library rather than on the Internet.

1. _____
2. _____
3. _____
4. _____
5. _____

Answer

Using the information from this section on Library Resources, you may have mentioned topics that might be found in back issues of local newspapers or periodicals, or in reference books that charge high subscription rates on the Internet. Also listed could be facts about obscure subjects or documents from the early to mid-20th century.

Going to the Experts

Sometimes, you can't find out what you need to know from a website or the library. The information might be very timely, such as interest rates on mortgages that change daily, or it just might not be published (such as someone's opinion on a given subject). In such a case, you need to find a person or people who have the information you are looking for.

Experts are simply those who know their subjects and can be relied upon to supply correct information. They might know about it because they have studied it or worked with it long enough to be considered highly informed. Getting information from an expert can be simple. You might just have to look up a number in the phone book and make a quick call. Or, it can involve a number of steps. You might need to do some research first to find your expert. That could mean asking around or using the resources of your library or the Internet. Once you have a name and contact information, you can proceed to gather information.

The great benefit of finding an expert you can trust, who has the facts you need, is that he or she can save you time. Instead of hunting for information from sources that may or may not yield what you are looking for, you have a reliable source. A loan officer at your bank will know exactly what the current mortgage rate is and be able to explain the difference in cost, long-term, between a 15- and a 20-year mortgage. Related questions may be answered without consulting other websites or print resources.

TIP

Recognizing that you don't have all the answers yourself is an important first step. Then you need to determine who or what you should consult and what questions to ask to find a solution.

Checking Credentials

You can't rely on information you get from a so-called "expert" until you determine that he or she has the proper credentials. Ask questions. Where is this expert getting his or her information? On what sources does the person rely? How is he or she qualified to provide you with the information you seek? For example, let's say Marty wants to know how many people used the picnic area in the city park this summer. She calls the Recreation and Parks Department and asks if someone can help her. The person on the phone puts Marty on hold, and then gives her a number to answer her question. Marty should ask where the number came from: Is it the officially recorded number of people who reserved picnic space and how many people were in their parties, or is it an estimate of the number of people based on counts in previous years?

Practice

Ted wants to stress the importance of recycling to his children. He constantly reminds them to put cans and plastic items in the recycling bins he's set up in the garage. One day his youngest daughter asks, "What do they do with this stuff anyway?" Ted doesn't really know, so he can't answer her question, but he suggests they research together to find out. Which is the best way for Ted and his daughter to get the information they need?

a. write a letter to the mayor of their town
b. look it up in the local newspaper
c. call or visit a local recycling center
d. check out their state's website

Answer

Someone at the recycling center, choice c, who works with the materials and prepares them before they leave the plant, probably has the answer. The mayor is probably not involved in details regarding what happens to the recycled materials after the local crew picks them up from homes and offices. The local paper and the state website might have something about recycling, but not the information Ted and his daughter need.

In Short

Your solutions and decisions are only as good as the information you use to make them. Sometimes you need only to deal with facts already known to you. In other instances, you may need to do some research.

The three best resources to consult are the Internet, the library, and other people (experts). Knowing how and when to use each type of resource can mean the difference between making an uninformed decision, and standing solidly behind the facts as you solve problems and decide among various options.

Skill Building Until Next Time

- If you've never used a meta-search engine, make a practice search. Compare your results with those from a resource you use frequently.
- Visit some sites mentioned in this lesson and see what each has to offer. Follow a few links that may be of interest to you.
- Before your next doctor's appointment, write some health-related questions you would like answered. Ask the expert during your exam.

8 ▶ EVALUATING FACTS

Get the facts, or the facts will get you. And when you get them, get them right, or they will get you wrong.

Dr. Thomas Fuller, British writer and physician (1654–1734)

LESSON SUMMARY
What's the difference between a fact and an opinion? Does someone's opinion about a subject carry as much weight as hard facts? In this lesson, we'll examine the difference between facts and opinions and how to make a distinction between accurate, objective information and the kind that's false or biased.

Many people believe that newspapers are good sources for current, factual information. But the last time you were in the supermarket checkout line, did you happen to notice any newspapers with stories about the impending end of the life on Earth, people who've had close encounters with aliens or been "abducted" by them, or an animal born with two human heads? Well, most of us are smart enough to know the difference between those kinds of newspapers, which are considered more entertainment than news, and the prize-winning papers that are widely accepted as trustworthy resources.

But there's more to determining accuracy and objectivity in informational sources than just knowing the difference between hard news reporting and superficial sensationalism. You need to develop a skeptical eye to spot the subtle differences between truthful, impartial resources and those that claim to be truthful and impartial before you can rely on any resource to help you make an important decision to solve a problem. Finding resources is important, it's true, but you have to figure out which you can trust and which you can't.

Fact Versus Opinion

Facts are objective statements that can be proven to be true. If a statement is true, then it's always true. For example, "Hawaii became a state in 1959." That's true because it's simple to verify that Hawaii did, indeed, join the United States in that year. An opinion, on the other hand, is a subjective statement based on personal beliefs. Therefore, it isn't always true for everyone. For example, "Hawaii is America's most beautiful state." You can tell this is based on a personal belief because the subjective word "beautiful" is used and the statement is open to debate. Lots of other people might disagree; they might choose their own or some other state as the most beautiful!

Practice

Label each statement **F** (fact) or **O** (opinion).

_____**1.** Sacagawea is the most important woman in American history.

_____**2.** Gravity pulls anything at or near Earth's surface toward the center of the planet.

_____**3.** The U. S. Constitution was adopted on September 17, 1787.

_____**4.** Trying to graduate from college in three years instead of four isn't a good idea for anyone.

_____**5.** Groundhog Day is always celebrated on February 2.

Answers

1. O, 2. F, 3. F, 4. O, 5. F.

TIP

Always remember that a fact can be verified. An opinion may be based on fact, but it's still someone's personal interpretation of the fact. Some experts try to make you think their interpretations are really facts.

Trusting the Source

Not everyone who gives out information is telling the truth. Pretty obvious, you think, and many times you are right. You probably don't take newspaper accounts of alien abductions seriously, even though you see them in print. But what about a documentary that purports to reveal the same thing? Can you be fooled by the delivery of the information, with fancy sets and a well-known actor as narrator, to believing what you might otherwise dismiss?

In order to trust the source of any information, you need to determine the agenda of the person or organization disseminating it. Are they simply trying to relay facts, or are they trying to get you to believe something or change your mind on a subject? It can be difficult to find a direct answer to that question; you can begin to get a clearer picture by looking into the following:

- **What are the author's credentials on this subject?** Is he or she qualified to write on the topic based on background or education? For some subjects, it is acceptable to use information obtained from a hobbyist, self-proclaimed expert, or enthusiast, if you can verify it elsewhere. However, most factual information should be obtained from a reputable source. And since you need to verify anyway, why not use information, for instance, derived from Yale University's Thomas Hardy Association, rather than from John Doe's personal web page paying homage to his favorite writer?

- **Does the author document sources?** Where do relevant facts and figures come from? If you are consulting print material, there should be footnotes and a bibliography of the author's sources. On the Internet, you may also find such documentation, or sources may be documented with links to other websites (see the next section "Evaluating Internet Information"). Even documentaries, to use a previous example, should cite sources in their credits.

- **Are the sources balanced and reputable?** Pages of footnotes are meaningless if they simply indicate that the author used untrustworthy sources, too. Check some of the sources to verify that they are accurate and unbiased. For example, a book on gun laws that relies heavily on material published by the National Rifle Association is not as reliable a source as another book on the subject that uses a wide variety of sources representing both sides of the issue.

- **What do others say about the individual writer or the group?** A quick way to check is to do an Internet search for the name of the author or group. The results can be revealing, but be sure to read with a critical eye. If you're searching for a person or group with a controversial view, you'll probably find detractors. A few skeptics shouldn't worry you, but pages of negative criticism might.

Practice

Terrell has been assigned a term paper that will test how well he and his class have learned research skills. He must write objectively on the subject of U.S. Military spending and has been given a list of possible sources for information. Which source or sources will provide the most objective information?

- **a.** Congressional Budget Office
- **b.** The U.S. Department of the Interior
- **c.** Alliance of Defense Contractors
- **d.** Center for World Peace

Answer

The Congressional Budget Office, choice **a**, would be the best place for Terrell to find balanced information. It's a non-partisan group that provides budget analysis to Congress, which must approve military spending. The U.S. Department of the Interior is America's primary conservation agency, and the Alliance of Defense Contractors and Center for World Peace organizations have very specific agendas, so they wouldn't be good sources for objective information on military spending.

Determining Bias

Bias is a preference that makes a person prejudiced. We often assume that authors of factual information are without bias. News articles by their very nature are intended to be objective reports of facts. The opinion of the writer shouldn't play a part in the reporting. But just like everyone else, writers have opinions about things and these opinions sometimes creep into their reporting. For example, newspaper and TV reporters are supposed to deliver the facts without giving an opinion, but you can't assume that they do. As a skeptical reader, be aware of word usage, and as a viewer, keep your eyes and ears open. Body language and voice inflection can tell a lot about the reporter's views on a subject.

Some TV news channels stress that their coverage of stories is balanced and fair, but many critics say newscasters are often biased in their reporting. In fact, many critics—and viewers—believe that certain channels are always for the "left" while others are always for the "right."

Watch and read the news from a variety of sources. Check for differences in story coverage. Which spent more time on a celebrity death or divorce than on peace talks or problems in the Middle East? Which skipped the Middle East stories altogether to give coverage to a local politician's hand-shaking opportunity that day? Try to find out more about the people who report the news. Are they former politicians or political speechwriters? Do they have affiliations with special interest groups? What, if any, are their biases?

Evaluating Internet Information

As discussed in the last lesson, anyone can publish on the Internet. It takes very little money or skill to create a website, so the existence and look of a site is no indication that it's a valuable resource. That being said, the Internet really can be a great resource for information—just don't assume that everything you read is truthful and unbiased. You have to learn to differentiate between authentic and bogus information.

Who Wrote It?

The first step in determining if Internet information is truthful and unbiased is to evaluate it in terms of authority. Ask three questions:

1. **"Who wrote or takes responsibility for this content?"** Look for the name and contact information of the author, who may be an individual or an organization—more than just an e-mail address. If no author is listed, you may discover who published it by removing the last part of the URL to the right of the last slash, and then clicking on *search*. If that doesn't work, remove the next part of the Web address, continuing from right to left until you reach the publisher's page. Does the publisher claim responsibility for the content or explain why the page exists? If not, you can't determine the authority of the site.

2. **"What are the qualifications of the person or group responsible for this page?"** (See the section on verifying an author's credentials earlier in the lesson.) Many people write daily blogs and may not have any know-how on the subject.

3. **"Can I verify the legitimacy of the person or group?"** This should be relatively easy to determine for well-known authors and groups who publish online. For others, you can contact them by e-mail, if an address is provided, and ask about credentials and legitimacy. But this isn't foolproof, so consider any whose legitimacy is difficult to verify as a source of opinion, not fact.

Practice

Which of the following web addresses are probably personal web pages?

    a. www.members.aol.com/jspinner582/

    b. www.stateuniversity.edu

    c. www.getthefacts.com/republican/~randyc/

    d. http://fightforrights.org

Answer

Choices **a** and **c** are most likely personal web pages. The tilde (~)in choice **c** gives it away as a personal page.

Judge the Accuracy of the Content

There are a few giveaways of marginal content. Review the website for the following:

1. Sources of factual information should be clearly listed so they can be verified elsewhere. Do not accept anything as fact that you can't verify at least three times, in three unique locations.

2. Factual information should come directly from its source. A statistic from the Wall Street Journal is more likely to be correct if you get it from their website, rather than rely on it as printed somewhere else. Always go to the source website (if one exists) or print material to check facts.

3. There should be no grammatical, spelling, or typographical errors. Not only do these errors indicate weak or nonexistent editing, but they can lead to inaccuracies in information.

Tales of a Web Page Address (URL)

- Businesses or others selling or promoting products or services, as well as news organizations, typically end in *.com* (the "com" means commercial).
- Informational websites, like those of a government, usually end in *.gov, .mil, .us,* or another country code, such as *.au* for Australia and *.uk* for the United Kingdom.
- Educational groups, from elementary schools to design schools to major universities, end in *.edu.*
- Non-profit organizations and groups that try to influence public opinion, such as the Democratic and Republican parties, end in *.org.*
- The most potentially unreliable information sources are personal web pages. Most are easy to identify—a tilde (~) in the address is a giveaway. But be careful, some URLs with *.edu* endings, usually indicating educational sites, also have a tilde and include a person's name. That's because some educational institutions offer free or low-cost web pages to their students, employees, and/or alumni. So be sure to look at the whole URL, not just part of it.

Check Dates

Legitimate websites typically include the date the site was written, when it was launched, and the last time it was updated. Without these dates, you cannot with any certainty use the information found on the site, especially if it is of a factual or statistical nature. If you have dates, ask yourself:

- Is the information current enough for my needs?
- If I need time-sensitive information, are the facts I found stale or do they represent the latest findings?
- If I don't need time-sensitive information, was this information placed on the Internet near the time it occurred?
- Was the page updated a relatively short time ago or could the author have abandoned it?

Use Links to Evaluate a Site

Most websites use links to help you move from their site to other web pages. These links may be used to document sources (think of them as the Internet equivalent of footnotes) or simply to take you to more information about the topic which may be of interest.

If there are links to other pages as sources, ask yourself the following:

- Do the links work?
- Are they to reliable sources or only to other locations on the same website?
- If they take you to more information on the subject, are they well chosen and well organized?
- Do the links represent other viewpoints?
- Do they indicate a bias?
- Are there links to directories? Are they discriminating or do they accept any and all sites?

If other pages link themselves to the page you are considering as a source, ask yourself:

- Who links to the page? (read all points of view if more than one may be found)
- How many links are there? (higher numbers may generally be a good sign)
- What kinds of sites link to it? (do they all represent the same point of view, giving the same information)

Verify Reproduced Information

If a website includes quotes, statistics, or other information purported to be from another source, check it for accuracy. Never assume that simply because the words or numbers are printed, they are correct. Quotes that have been retyped may contain errors, have been deliberately altered, or be complete fakes. The best way to check is to find the information somewhere else, preferably at its source.

For example, Chuck reads a website that claims Earth's human population is decreasing. It cites an expert who is quoted in *Scientific American* magazine. Chuck should check his public library, which probably has back issues or a subscription to the magazine's online archives that he can search for free.

Keep in mind that material reproduced from another publication, if it is legitimate, will probably include both a link to the original source (if it's online), and copyright information and permission to reproduce or reprint. If there is a link, be certain it is from the original source.

Practice

Label each statement **T** (true) or **F** (false).

___ **1.** Because anyone can publish on the Internet, it's hard to know if what you read is true.

___ **2.** You only need to check the credentials of individuals or groups who write print materials.

___ **3.** All TV and newspaper reporters are unbiased.

___ **4.** Links on a website are supposed to be like the footnotes in print materials.

___ **5.** As long as a website quotes a famous person, you know what you read is true.

Answer

1. T, 2. F, 3. F, 4. T, 5. F.

In Short

Thinking critically means being armed with accurate information. It's vital to evaluate information to see if it's subjective or objective, fact or opinion, accurate or false, and/or biased. You have to look at the source of the information, or the author(s). Can you trust the source and the credentials of the author(s)? Keep a skeptical eye out for opinion posing as fact, inferior research and documentation, and bias from every source.

When using the Internet, which can be a hazardous place to find information, you have to evaluate any Web page you come across in your research. It's important to find the author and dates for each website, as well as judge the accuracy of its content, and use its links to evaluate even further what you read. Your critical-thinking skills are enhanced when you learn to evaluate the information you receive. Think for yourself! Never assume that something is true without checking it out, and don't take for granted that any source's viewpoint is unbiased.

TIP

Never accept statements at face value. Every statement should be carefully evaluated to find the truth. Remember, truthfulness and reasoning aren't the same thing.

Skill Building Until Next Time

- Read a magazine article and note its author. Does the magazine itself tell you anything about his or her credentials? Look up the author on the Internet to see if you can find what expertise, if any, he or she has in the subject.
- The next time you hear a fact on a TV news story, try to substantiate it. Remember the rule of threes: Find it in three more sources before accepting it as fact.

LESSON 9

► PERSUASION TECHNIQUES

If you would persuade, you must appeal to interest rather than intellect.

Benjamin Franklin, American writer, statesman,
and scientist (1706-1790)

LESSON SUMMARY

People are always trying to influence your choices and decisions. "Vote for me!" "Buy my product!" Those are out-in-the-open persuasions; you know what someone is trying to get you to do. But there are subtle ways to persuade, and in this lesson, you'll learn to recognize both kinds used in speaking, writing, and advertising. And you'll discover how you can use those same techniques to your advantage.

Persuasion is the art of using argument, reasoning, or influence to change what people do or the way they think. Everyone uses persuasion techniques, even you. As a kid, you may have tried to persuade your parents to let you stay up an hour later, buy you a toy you wanted, or let you sleep later.

As you grew up, you continued to use persuasion. Maybe you decided to ask for a raise because you felt you'd earned it. So you went to your boss with examples of good work you'd done for the company. In other words, you tried to make the boss think a certain way—that you were a great employee who deserved a raise. But instead of agreeing to a raise, the boss explained that things weren't so good at corporate headquarters. He said stock prices were down and, "I know you understand, being one of our best and brightest, why we can't increase your salary at this time." Your boss turned the tables by using persuasion, including evidence and flattery, to change your mind about the raise!

People also use persuasion in more organized ways. Political groups and advertisers try to influence your vote and how you spend your money. Persuasion that is exceptionally systematic and organized is known as propaganda, which uses multiple techniques to attempt to bring about a change in a group of people.

A History of the Art of Persuasion

Aristotle studied and taught philosophy, science, and public speaking in Greece during the fourth century BCE. In one of his most famous works, *The Art of Rhetoric* (meaning "persuasion through language"), he stated that the ideal form of argument was an appeal to reason, called *logos*. But he acknowledged two other powerful techniques, *ethos*—an appeal to character—and *pathos*—an appeal to emotions. These same techniques are still in use today.

- *Logos:* **Appeal to Reason.** This works because most people think they are reasonable and logical. Someone makes an argument based on the theory that "any logical, reasonable person would agree!" He or she might contend, "Of course, we **all** know that if we don't do X now, then Y will surely be the result!"

- *Pathos:* **Appeal to Emotion.** Aristotle understood that not everything we do is based on logic. We all have emotions, or feelings, and this kind of persuasion can work in three different ways. First, someone can express his or her own feelings on a subject, hoping to influence others. Second, someone can try to get an emotional reaction from listeners in order to persuade them. Third, someone can both express his or her own emotions and at the same time arouse those feelings in listeners. For example, environmental groups use this approach by saying things like, "Thousands of baby seals are brutally murdered for their skins, in front of their horrified mothers. Shouldn't we act now to save these innocent creatures?"

- *Ethos:* **Appeal to Character.** Here, Aristotle refers to the character of a speaker, who must be seen as worthy in the eyes of an audience. In other words, for a person's art of persuasion to work, others must see him or her as trustworthy, honest, and/or intelligent. That way he or she earns credibility as someone who can be relied on and believed. Here's an example: "I spent 12 years in the U.S. Navy, serving our country with honor. I learned how the military operates and am the only candidate with direct, personal contact with our armed services. So I know better than any other candidate how to maintain and improve our military to make it the best in the world."

Practice

Label each statement either **L** (logos), **P** (pathos), or **E** (ethos).

_____ 1. Fellow stockholders, we need Ned Cash on our Board of Directors. His many years as finance director for New City make him the ideal person to help stabilize our company in this global market.

_____ 2. It just makes sense to buy from a superstore. Things cost less when you buy in bulk, and you don't run out of stuff as often. That saves gas because you make fewer trips to the store!

_____ 3. Adopt a pet. Come to the shelter and look into the eyes of any cat or dog. All it wants is a loving home and a new lease on life. Please, say "I care."

Answers

1. **E.** Ned's experience makes him seem highly qualified, so listeners assume he's worthy of their trust and their votes.
2. **L.** a logical argument, appealing to reasoning ability
3. **P.** uses emotion to persuade

Pathos

The most frequently seen of Aristotle's three persuasion techniques is *pathos,* or emotional influence. For example, using scare tactics is common.

Scare Tactics

Here's an example of scare tactics: Linda receives a phone call from a stranger, asking if she knows if her local emergency response units are prepared to handle a terrorist attack. He describes the aftermath of a bombing, with all of its destruction and bloodshed, and tells her that her local medical community, firefighters, and law enforcement aren't ready to respond adequately. He goes on to describe the chaos that would ensue due to the inadequate response. Then, he asks for a donation to a national organization that he says can provide funding for local emergency response units. Linda is so frightened by the phone call that she gives the caller her credit card number, authorizing him to charge a $50 donation to the organization he represents. The caller persuaded her to give money to a group she never heard of, and which actually might not exist, because he successfully used scare tactics.

If you ever feel afraid after hearing someone speak, watching a TV ad, reading something, or browsing the Internet, put aside your emotions and think logically. Did the material aim at getting this emotional response from you? Did the speaker or writer mean to scare you in order to persuade you to do/buy/think something?

Pity

Evoking pity is another example of the pathos technique. Someone tries to make others feel sorry for him or her, hoping they'll do something, give money, or think a certain way out of pity. Some examples are TV and magazine ads that show hungry children surrounded by flies, panhandlers who tell passersby that they haven't eaten in days, and holiday news stories about poor families with no money to buy gifts for their children.

Flattery

Flattery, another form of pathos, makes people feel good about themselves, by complimenting their intelligence, good taste, or some other characteristic. This form of persuasion is important when trying to make a personal connection, so advertisers use it often. For example, "Because you're smart, you care about your health." The listener or reader is supposed to agree that, "Yes, I'm smart, so I care about my health." Then this smart person is expected to believe that a certain brand of food or over-the-counter drugs is what all smart, healthy people should buy.

Practice

Which is NOT an example of a persuasion technique?
  a. Give generously to our holiday fund. A homeless child will have a special present and a warm meal, thanks to you.
  b. Smart people like you know a good deal when you see one. So head on down to Toby's Togs for our 50% off sale.
  c. Home invasions are on the rise! How can you feel safe in your own home? Call *SAY-fty First* today for the best home security system available! Just $29 a month after initial installation fee.
  d. Cinema One is open seven days a week.

Answer

The correct answer is choice **d**. It's just a statement of fact, not a way of persuading you to choose that theater over any others.

TIP

Look closely at people's word choices as they try to influence your thinking. Do advertisers say you'll look "slim" or "skinny" in their clothes? Do TV reporters refer to a car crash as an "accident" or a "disaster"? Has there been an "incident" or a "threat"?

Persuasion and the Written Word

Writers use many tactics to persuade their readers. Known as rhetorical devices, these techniques subtly show the reader that the writer's point of view should be theirs, too. Here are six of the most common such devices, with definitions and examples.

1. **Rhetorical question:** implies that the answer is so obvious that there is no answer required. It persuades without making an argument.
   Example: Can we really expect our teachers to maintain a high standard of professionalism when we won't pay them a fair wage?

2. **The Rule of Three:** based on the theory that people remember things when they are listed in threes, it can be used to repeat the same thing exactly, the same idea said three different ways, or three items that belong together.
   Examples: "Stop, look, and listen"; "The most important factor in selling real estate is location, location, location"; "Is your car old? rusting? ready to be replaced?"

3. **Emotional language:** uses adjectives to get the reader to feel a certain way.
   Example: Management won't stop these cutbacks until all our children go hungry. Then they will close the plant and leave us unemployed and out on the street.

4. **Hyperbole:** the use of exaggeration for extravagant effect; often humorous.
   Example: The lines in my bank are so slow. Only the tellers who fail their training get jobs there.

5. **Sound patterns:** meant to get the reader's attention and cause him or her to remember content better; some of a number of different patterns are: rhyming, alliteration (repeating the same sound at the beginning of words),

consonance (repeating the same consonant sound), and assonance (the repetition of vowel sounds).
   Examples: sweet smell of success; dime a dozen; plain Jane

6. **Comparisons:** show a relationship between two unlike items by metaphor (uses verb "to be"), simile (uses "like" or "as"), or personification (gives human qualities to animals or objects).
   Examples: His eyes are searchlights, looking for any sign of recognition; She's as quiet as a mouse; The Moon smiled down as we walked away.

Practice

List the rhetorical devices used in the following paragraph:

"In closing, let me state that a vote for Sheuh Ling is <u>a vote for a perfect world</u>.
                                             1
She is <u>smart, savvy, and successful</u>. She
              2
knows how to get things done. The other candidates want to return us to a time when <u>jobs were scarce, people were scared</u>,
                                 3
and government was looking over everyone's shoulder. Let's not let that happen. <u>Why turn back the clock</u> when we can
                    4
move forward into a brighter future?"

Answer

1. "a vote for a perfect world"—hyperbole

2. "smart, savvy, and successful" —Rule of Three

3. "jobs were scarce, people were scared . . ." —emotional language

4. "why turn back the clock . . ."—rhetorical question

Implementing Persuasion Techniques

The art of persuasion isn't all about cleverly tricking people into changing their actions or way of thinking. It can also be used in positive ways to get what you want in life. For example, at a job interview, it's your mission to persuade someone to hire you. You won't be preying on fears or asking for pity, but you'll use your choice of words (spoken and written in your resume), your appearance, your behavior, and your body language to convince the person to offer you a job.

What else can you do to persuade people? Here's a list of some ways. Not all will work in every situation, so use your critical-thinking skills to evaluate each situation and choose accordingly.

1. **Grab people's attention.** Act in a way that'll get someone to listen to you. That means being respectful, diplomatic (no yelling or belittling), modest but confident, and reasonable.
2. **Be sincere.** It's critical not only to sound convincing, but to convince people that what you're saying is believable. Use evidence and examples to prove that your claims and appeals are true, and the right way to go.
3. **Be personal.** Know who you're trying to persuade, and then use what you know about them in your appeal. Explain exactly what they'll get out of it if they see things your way. Answer the question "what's in it for me?" before they have a chance to ask it!
4. **Show concern.** Is your audience worried or afraid about something? State their concern so they see that you share it, even if you really have a different view. "I can see you're worried about global warming, and it's a real concern to me, too."
5. **Ask for what you want.** Be direct about the result you want. For example, "Now you can see why there's an urgent need to save the rainforest, and why we need you to donate to the cause today."

Practice

Your friend wants to vacation in the Bahamas this winter, but you want to ski. You found a great deal on a ski package, including hotel and airfare, but it requires two people traveling together to get the reduced rates. How do you present this information to convince your friend?

_____

_____

_____

_____

_____

Answer

There are many ways, but you might say:

"I know you want to go the Bahamas for the warm weather, but there won't be many people our age at that resort. I'm worried we will get bored after sitting on the beach all day. The ski lodge I looked into is directly targeting 20-somethings. They will give us a low rate on hotel, airfare, and lift tickets, plus they are throwing a free party every night for everyone who bought the package deal."

Persuasive Advertising

There are two kinds of advertising. Informative marketing simply seeks to familiarize consumers with a product or service by reminding them of an existing product/service or introducing a new one. Persuasive advertising aims to manipulate consumer spending habits and make them want to buy a product or service by appealing to their senses, emotions, or intellect. Some common persuasive techniques include:

- **Sensory appeal:** a perfect looking product, an exciting background color, a catchy slogan or jingle
- **Sex appeal:** pictures, voice, word choice, attractive models
- **Group appeal:** can be a snob (makes consumer believe purchase will place him/her in ranks of the elite), an Average Joe (reverse snob appeal—you will be like everyone else, won't stand out), "in" group (you will be more popular or cooler if you buy), or a bandwagon (you want what everyone else has)

- **Authority:** uses the endorsements of celebrities or other powerful people; you will be like them if you use the product or service
- **Scientific or statistical:** uses figures, experiments, impressive-sounding ingredients, and other proof that product is superior
- **Flattery:** compliments your intelligence, looks, or other characteristic to make you to want to buy the product or service
- **Unfinished claim:** says product or service is better, but doesn't tell you what it is better than

You need to know that an ad is trying to persuade you before you can resist it. It's not usually too hard because advertisers tend to use the same kinds of claims and appeals repeatedly.

You can use an evaluation form, like the one shown, to check out ads. Once you understand what you're looking for, you'll be able to evaluate ads you see and hear without needing a form. Instead of being duped by persuasion, you'll see the words and images for what they are: attempts to manipulate you.

Persuasive Advertising Evaluation

Product _____

Appeal(s) 1. _____ how accomplished _____

2. _____ how accomplished _____

Claim(s) 1. _____ how accomplished _____

2. _____ how accomplished _____

What is effective about the appeal(s)? _____

What is effective about the claim(s)? _____

In Short

Throughout history, people have had a need to get others to change their minds. Writers, politicians, business people, advertisers, and special interest groups, to name a few, use persuasion techniques to manipulate their audiences. Therefore, you encounter (and use) many of these tactics every day. When you recognize them and understand how they work, you can not only resist them when you need to, but use them to your advantage.

TIP

Don't be fooled by ads with "average" people, who look and act like friends and neighbors. The ads want you to think you'll love the product those people are using because they're just like you. Remember, even if they're not professional actors, which many are, they're still getting paid to influence you!

Skill Building Until Next Time

- Go through the latest issue of your favorite magazine. Pick out two advertisements and fill out an evaluation (like the previous one) for each.
- Choose two familiar TV commercials. List the different kinds of persuasive advertising techniques used in each. Which technique do you think would convince most viewers?

10 ▶ THE NUMBERS GAME

Figures don't lie, but liars figure.

Mark Twain, American writer and humorist (1835–1910)

LESSON SUMMARY

Numbers are facts, so numbers are always true, right? Well, not always. Sometimes people use numerical information incorrectly, either innocently or with a motive to mislead. In this lesson, we'll explore some common ways numbers are misused, including incorrectly gathering the figures, drawing the wrong conclusion, and misrepresenting the data.

We're bombarded with facts and figures every day—numerical information about what's going on in the world, who we should vote for, what we should buy, and even what we should think. The problem is, facts and figures aren't always factual. You've probably heard the old saying, "numbers don't lie." Well, they do, or rather the people who use them do!

Numbers are manipulated all the time, whether by deliberate misuse, negligence, or plain incompetence, so that what we see, hear, and read isn't always the truth. If we rely on numbers in statistics, polls, or percentages as a basis for decisions and opinions, we could be making a serious mistake. After all, people who work with numbers and those who analyze or interpret them are people. They may be biased, less than competent, or negligent, so you have to be just as concerned with the sources and quality of numbers as you are with words.

Numbers can be misused. It all happens in one, or both, of two key areas. First, numbers must be gathered. If they are collected incorrectly, or by someone with an agenda or bias, you need to know that. Second, numbers must be analyzed or interpreted. Again, this process can be done incorrectly, or misused by an individual or group. Once you learn what to look for in these two areas, you can evaluate the numerical data you encounter and rely on it only when it is objective and correct.

Manipulating Surveys

Authors, advertisers, businesses, and politicians rely on surveys, polls, and other statistics to make their points of view appear more credible and important. The problem is, it's just as easy to mislead with numbers as with words. Numbers must be gathered correctly so they can be trusted. Here are a few examples, including how numbers are manipulated so they can't be trusted.

A survey questions a small number of people and applies the results to a large number of people. An accurate survey should,

1. **Use an appropriate sample population** that is
   - **large enough**—if the sample number is too low, it won't be representative of a larger population; asking just two people if they like a new ice cream flavor and finding that one person does doesn't mean that 50% of all ice cream eaters, a number in the millions, will like the flavor.
   - **similar to the target population**—if the target population includes ages 10–60, your sample can't be taken just from a junior high school

   - **random**—asking only union members about labor laws is not random; asking one hundred people whose phone numbers were picked by a computer is

2. **Remain un-biased.** Ask objective questions and create a non-threatening, non-influencing atmosphere. Compare, "Do you think people should be allowed to own dangerous firearms if they have innocent young children at home?" to "Do you think people should be allowed to exercise their Second Amendment right to own a firearm?" Also, if the person asking the question is wearing a "Gun Control Now!" or "Gun Freedom Now!" button, his or her bias pollutes the environment and will influence the answers received.

Imagine an ad that reads, "Eighty percent of respondents in a recent survey liked Smilebright toothpaste better than Brightsmile." The high percentage is meant to convince readers that most people prefer Smilebright, so you will, too. But how was that percentage figured? The survey consisted of asking five people, who already said they preferred a gel-type toothpaste, whether they liked Smilebright or Brightsmile. There was no random sampling—everyone had the same preference, which is probably not true for a larger population.

Practice

List two things wrong with the following survey:

The head of a stock exchange company sent a questionnaire to the firm's employees. It began with an introduction, in which he praised the work everyone was doing to help the company grow, then asked, "Do you believe the federal government has the right to set limits on the bonuses given to hard-working stock brokers in America?"

_____

_____

Answer

The survey population isn't random because it only went to people in the firm. Both the introductory material and question show bias—complimenting employees for being hard workers, then using the word "hard-working" to stress that those answering the question would be the ones affected by any government action.

TIP

Remember, surveys can't prove anything with 100% certainty unless the sample questions 100% of the population.

Correlation Studies

Once numbers are gathered, they must be interpreted or evaluated, and this step affords many opportunities to distort the truth. For example, researchers often do correlation studies to find out if a link exists between two sets of data. Here are two questions someone might use for a correlation study:

- Is there a connection between the full moon and an increase in birth rates?
- Does having a high IQ indicate that you will have a high income level?

Imagine that research at five area hospitals shows that during a full moon, an average of 4% more babies are born than on nights with no full moon. You could then say there's a small but positive correlation between full moons and birth rates. But many studies have shown that any correlation is really due to chance. No evidence has been found to support the theory that the

---

Margin of Error

Most survey results end with a statement such as "there is a margin of error of three percentage points." What does this mean? It tells how confident the surveyors are that their results are correct. The lower the percentage, the greater their confidence. A 3% margin of error means that the sample population of the survey could be different from the general population by 3% in either direction. Let's say a survey concluded that "55% of Americans want to vote for members of the Supreme Court." If there is a 3% margin of error, the results could be 58%, 52%, or anywhere in between, if you conducted the identical survey asking another group of people.

Knowing the margin of error is important, especially in political polls. Imagine a headline that reads, "Smith's lead slips to 58%; Manotti gaining momentum at 37%." The accompanying article states that last week, the results were 61% to 34%, with a 4% margin of error. That means there's really no difference between the two polls. No one is "slipping" or "gaining momentum." The margin of error tells the real story; the news article is wrong.

moon's phases affect human behavior in any way. So, even though you found a positive correlation, it doesn't necessarily mean there's a cause-and-effect relationship between the two elements in the study.

For the second question, if a study showed that Americans with the top 5% of IQ scores made an average of $22,000 a year, while those in the middle 5% made an average of $40,000, you would say there is a negative correlation between IQ and income levels. To describe the results of the study, you could say that there is no evidence that IQ determines income level. In other words, you do not need to have a high IQ to make a lot of money.

This conclusion is obvious. But let's look at how these same correlation study results can be used to come up with a ridiculous conclusion. The second example shows that there is no connection between a high IQ and a high income level. Is that the same as saying that "the dumber you are, the more money you will make?" Of course it isn't. This type of conclusion shows one of the dangers of correlation studies. Even if the study uses accurate data, the way in which it is interpreted can be wrong, and even foolish. When you encounter a correlation study, as with survey and poll results, do not assume the numbers and conclusion are correct. Ask questions, and look at supporting data. Does the study make sense? Or does it seem too convenient for the advertiser/politician/reporter/author who is using it? Think critically, and do not rely on anyone's numbers until you determine they are true and valid.

Practice

Which is an appropriate conclusion to draw from the following correlation study?

Researchers wanted to know if children's TV viewing affected reading habits. They conducted a study which showed that over 33% of homes with children between the ages of one and six had a TV on most or all of the time. Children in these "heavy-television households" watched TV more and read less than other children do.

a. If you own a TV, your six-year-old child will not want to read.

b. Children in homes with no TV are better readers.

c. Watching TV most of the time may cause one in three young children to read less.

d. Children who watch only educational programs read more than children who watch other kinds of shows.

Answer

Choice **c** is the only conclusion that can be drawn from the study. There was no information about educational programs (choice **d**) or no-TV homes (choice **b**), and we don't know if your TV is on most or all the time (choice **a**).

Statistics

Statistics is simply a mathematical science that gathers information about a population so that population may be described usefully. Statistics are often used to draw conclusions and make decisions based on that information. So, what's the problem?

Statistics are complicated and their problems can be numerous. In general, though, problems with statistics are similar to those of other types of numerical data; namely, they can be gathered, analyzed, and/or interpreted incorrectly, or mishandled by someone with a bias. Let's look at two common problems with statistics.

- **Is it meaningful?** Many parents worry when they hear that the average baby walks at 13 months. They may conclude that something must be wrong with their 18-month-old who is still crawling. But, studies have proven that at age two, there are no developmental differences between early walkers and babies who walk later. So the statistic is not meaningful; there is nothing abnormal about an 18-month-old who still crawls. Here is another example. When national standardized test scores were analyzed, it was concluded that since students from wealthy communities had higher scores, they were smarter than students in poorer communities. Is that a meaningful, accurate conclusion? Probably not; it doesn't take into account the many other variables that can explain lower test scores, such as teacher quality, less test preparation, fatigue, and even breakfast on the day of testing.

TIP

Always check the source of data. Is the source credible? Look for another source that gives similar data to strengthen the credibility.

Practice

Evidence shows that more car accidents occur on days with clear weather than on days when it is snowing. Can you conclude that it is safer to drive when it is snowing? Why, or why not?

_____

_____

_____

_____

_____

Answer

No, other factors influence this statistic, such as the fact that more people are probably on the road in clear weather than snowy weather.

- **Is the statistic misrepresented?** Ask yourself: is the statistic given in such a way that it misrepresents the data collected—does it make the data sound better or worse than it really is? Suppose a survey is run to find out how many children live below the poverty line. The results are reported on the news: "80% of all children

live above the poverty line." So, what about the 20% who live below it? The 80% sounds good, but shifts the focus away from the millions of children who are poor.

Practice

Researchers found that 98% of juvenile offenders committing serious crimes watch violent TV shows on a regular basis. If you are an advocate for a reduction in TV violence, how would you use this statistic? What if you were an advocate for freedom of expression on television?

_____

_____

_____

_____

_____

Answer

As an advocate for a reduction in TV violence, you would probably say, "Watching violence on TV turns our young people into criminals." If you were an advocate for freedom of expression on television, you might find out the real number of young people in the 2%. Let's say it is 3 million. You might conclude that "millions of children watch violent programs regularly, and they don't end up as criminals."

- **Are all the facts there?** Another common way to manipulate statistics is to leave out key information. Let's say a bicycle company claims it's edging out its competitor with higher sales. It did have a 50% increase in sales, compared with only a 25% increase for the competitor, but is that "edging out" claim valid? You need more information to know. Suppose the competitor sold 2,000 bikes last year and 2,400 this year; the other company sold 40 bikes last year and 60 this year. Edging out the competition? Hardly!

When you hear a statistic in an advertisement, a political speech, a newspaper article, or other source, remember that it is not necessarily true. Then, ask yourself three questions: Is the statistic meaningful? Does it deliberately misrepresent the data collected? Does it give you all the information you need to evaluate it? Thinking critically about statistics will help you to avoid making the wrong conclusions, or relying on information that is faulty or simply untrue.

Practice

What's wrong with this statement?

The teachers in our school system are better off now; they earn an average of $25,000 a year.

_____

_____

_____

_____

_____

Answer

We don't have enough information—these teachers are better off compared with what? The salaries of teachers in other school systems in the state? In the nation? What's the cost of living in the area? The teachers could be worse off if $25,000 is not worth what it was last year or five years ago. We also don't know if teachers' salaries cover just a standard 180-day school year or if they have to do after-school and summer programs, or if their total earnings come from teaching alone or if they "earn" at other jobs to supplement their teaching income.

TIP

Never trust numbers alone to prove a point. Ask yourself, "Why should I believe these statistics?" Always look for some other kind of evidence or an example to reinforce the figures.

In Short

It is just as easy to deceive with numbers as it is with words. Surveys, studies, and statistics are conducted and interpreted by researchers who might have a bias, or simply lack the skills necessary to do their jobs properly. Therefore, it is important to evaluate numbers before accepting them as truth. Ask questions about how the information was gathered, what its margin of error is, and how meaningful it is. Does the conclusion make sense, or does it seem to distort the findings? Thinking critically about the many numbers you encounter will help you to rely only on information that is objective and accurate.

Skill Building Until Next Time

- Watch a news broadcast and listen for the results of a survey or poll. Does the newscaster tell the margin of error? Why is it important to know this number?
- Look for a print or article that includes a statistic. Why was it included? Does it seem accurate and objective? How else could the advertiser or writer have made the point without using numbers?

11 ▶ CHECKING YOUR EMOTIONS

The sign of an intelligent people is their ability to control emotions by the application of reason.

Marya Mannes, American author and critic (1904–1990)

LESSON SUMMARY

What part do emotions play in the decision-making process? That's what this lesson is all about. You'll discover that if emotional responses are accepted and used properly, they can be a useful element in critical thinking. But if they're used inappropriately, emotions can make things even worse!

Many people believe that objective thinking and decision making involves only the brain. After all, *objective* means "not influenced by emotions." But can you, and more importantly, should you, completely ignore your feelings when you are making decisions? You may be surprised to learn that the answer is "No!"

Feelings, or emotions, have a place in critical thinking, just as logic does. But decisions should never be made based on feelings alone, and some emotions are best left out of the process. Critical thinkers acknowledge their emotions and understand how they can influence decisions, and then take control of when and where any such emotions should become part of the process.

When Emotions Take Over the Decision-Making Process

Decision-making is a systematic, conscious process that seems to leave no room for feelings. But you can probably think of many decisions you have had to make recently in which you had strong feelings that influenced your outcome. Perhaps you had to decide whether to order dessert when you were out for dinner. You ordered the cheesecake because it is a favorite, ignoring the fact that you were trying to lower your cholesterol level. Or, you left work early because you had tickets to a ball game, even though you had a big project due the next day.

It doesn't matter if you're making a major decision, like whether to buy a car, or a minor one, like whether to have fries with your burger; the decision-making process is similar. In preceding lessons, you examined the steps in the process. Let's review them:

1. Recognize the problem.
2. Define the problem.
3. Focus observation to learn more about the problem.
4. Brainstorm possible solutions.
5. Choose a solution(s) and set goals.
6. Troubleshoot any problems that get in the way of your goal(s).
7. Try the solution and assess your results.
8. Use, modify, or reject the solution. Repeat the process if necessary.

You probably noticed there wasn't any step that said, "Determine how you feel about the problem or decision, and let your emotions rule." So what role, if any, do emotions have in the process? The answer is, a balanced role: Emotions shouldn't be ignored, nor should they be used as your sole criteria. When you recognize and define a problem, also recognize and define any feelings you might have. For example, you might think, "This whole situation makes me nervous, and I don't feel like I even want to deal with it!" Or you might think, "I'm excited about this. I want to get going!" Don't act on your feelings, just acknowledge them.

Here's an example of what can happen when someone lets emotions rule. Guy wants to go to college to get a degree in design, but he doesn't want to graduate after four years with a huge debt. His goal is to find a school that offers a great education without charging too much in tuition and other fees. He applies to three schools, and they all accept him. The first has a strong design department, the best reputation of the three, and fees within his budget. The second offers him a scholarship. The third costs more than the first, but his best friend is enrolling there. Logic would conclude that the first two schools offer compelling reasons for attending. The academic strengths and strong reputation of the first are good reasons to choose it, and although the second may be a notch down in quality, it would cost him practically nothing to attend. The third school has only one thing going for it: Guy's friend goes there. Guy picks the third school, a choice of emotion over logic.

TIP

If you discover that your emotions do get in the way of solving a problem, use them as a learning tool. Study what triggered a particular emotion so you can prevent it from getting in the way of reasoning in the future.

Practice

Which was decided by emotion alone?

a. Sandy used leftovers from last night's dinner to make her lunch.

b. Josef upgraded his cell phone because he needed features that allowed him to take photos and e-mail them for his job.

c. Sasha needed a new computer, so she read reviews, then bought the same brand she had been using.

d. When Ron moved into his small studio apartment, he needed a TV, so he bought a six-foot-long flat-screen TV for the wall.

Answer

Choice **d** is an emotion-driven decision. It's not logical for Ron to buy such a large, expensive TV for such a small apartment. (Neighbors might complain about the noise through the wall, too.) He most likely bought the TV because of how it makes him feel, or how he feels about it. Reasoning didn't come into play.

Bias and Stereotyping

Biases are preferences or beliefs that keep someone from being impartial or fair-minded. Stereotypes are generalized opinions or prejudiced attitudes about a group of people. Having a bias or stereotyping people keeps you from having an open mind and gets in the way of making logical decisions as you solve problems. You need to recognize and control your emotions, rather than letting them control you.

Here are two examples:

- **Bias:** Marta is a member of the town council. This week she must vote on a proposal that will bring much-needed revenue to the town, but will significantly reduce her friend's property value. The friend supported Marta's run for office and contributed to her campaign. Marta's bias is her feeling of loyalty toward her friend.

If Marta votes "no" on the proposal, she will make her decision based on friendship, not on the best interest of the town she was elected to serve.

- **Stereotyping:** A study was done of a certain doctor's habit of writing prescriptions for painkillers. It found that 75% of the prescriptions were written for male patients, although the doctor's practice was 50% male and 50% female. When asked about the discrepancy, the doctor remarked, "Females have a lower pain threshold. They should tolerate pain better, and stop relying on drugs." This doctor stereotyped women as being weaker and so their complaints of pain weren't as valid as men's. His stereotyping prevented him from making logical decisions and from adequately treating half of his patients.

Practice

Which are examples of bias or stereotyping?

1. I want to help, so I'll bake cookies for the school party.
2. Thank you, but we can't let the children eat cookies! People who do end up fat and unhealthy.
3. I like this blue sweater better than that green one.
4. Oh, he's nice, but I'd never go out with him; he's a college dropout!
5. Our team did a fantastic job, but your team got lucky, so we didn't win.

Answer

The answers are **2, 4,** and **5.** Choices **2** and **4** stereotype groups of people; choice **5** shows bias by downplaying the accomplishment of the other team. Although choice **3** is an opinion, it only shows a preference, not a bias.

TIP

Ask yourself, "How would I feel about this if I weren't letting my own views and beliefs affect my thinking?"

Making Decisions Under Stress

Stress can affect both physical and mental health, affecting the ability to think critically, solve problems, and make sound decisions. There is no way to control every potentially stressful situation that we may encounter; time pressures at work, lack of information, information overload, and aggressive individuals are things that we have to deal with from time to time whether we want to or not. What we can control is how we deal with stress and how we let it affect us.

When you are under too much stress, or you don't deal with the stressors that are affecting you, it will affect the way you make decisions. Some of the most common effects are:

- **Inability to recognize or understand a problem.** When stressed, it is difficult to access stored information quickly, if at all. Short-term memory is affected. You may incorrectly identify something as a problem when in fact it is not.
- **Difficulty brainstorming and setting reasonable goals.** When you do not accurately recognize the problem, and you have trouble concentrating, you may come up with a quick or irrational solution. You tend to think only about the immediate future, so planning is difficult and decisions are often made quickly.
- **Inability to assess the solution.** If you are having trouble taking in information, you will not be able to see if your solution works. A short-term view of everything may keep you from being concerned with the implications of your solution.

Taking part in an auction is an example of decision making under stress. Imagine that two people are interested in the same 100-year-old china plate. They've both seen the same kind of plate at other auctions and in antique shops, selling for about $50. So the two shoppers set a limit, even if only in their minds, of the price they're willing to pay for the plate. Then, the bidding begins. When several people want the same item, excitement builds and stressed bidders can be carried away by "auction fever." The winning bid could be over $100, more than double what the two bidders know the plate is worth. Reason and logic, when faced with stress, take a back seat to emotion.

How could both people have eliminated the stress and bid reasonably? They could have done just one simple thing: recognize what they could control, and exercise control over it. In this case, they could have set a price they wouldn't go over before the auction began, and stuck to it. But what about a more complicated issue, like refinancing a mortgage?

Barb filed refinancing papers three weeks ago and set a date for the closing. When she arrived at the closing, the loan officer told her that the interest rate had gone up a point, so she'd have to pay a higher rate. In this very stressful situation, Barb must make a decision. If she allows stress to take over, she'll probably do one of two things: tell the loan officer to forget it, or say nothing and continue with the closing even though the rate is higher. But if Barb recognizes what she has control over, she'll ask questions before making any move. For example, she could ask, "How does this rate compare with the one I'm already paying? What will my new payment be, as opposed to my old one? Can you waive the closing costs to help me save money?" In this situation, taking control means getting information.

A good rule to follow is this: Don't act until you understand the situation. Even if you're stressed, you can check your emotions and make good decisions.

Practice

List some of the effects of stress that can get in the way of decision making.

_____

_____

_____

_____

_____

Answer

Your answers might include some of the following: inability to concentrate; weak short-term memory; focus on the present, rather than the future; tendency to make snap judgments; difficulty accessing stored information; trouble taking in new information.

Watch Out for Ego

Some friends decide to go hiking in the mountains. They're all inexperienced hikers, so they choose an easy trail. Half way up the trail, a storm rolls in and it gets darker as a torrential downpour begins. Most of the group decides to head back down the trail, but two people decide to keep going. They laugh about the "quitters," and boast that a storm can't hold them back. Instead of thinking rationally, they let their egos make the decision so they'll appear strong and fearless. Unfortunately, they put themselves, and whoever will have to come and rescue them, at risk of serious harm.

Every individual should have a healthy vision of his or her abilities, strengths, and shortcomings. Trouble comes when that vision is inflated and it becomes a part of the decision-making process. The two hikers' choice to continue hiking and to ignore their own limitations was based on ego.

Business people can also get into trouble with their egos when they worry too much about how they appear to others. For example, a shop owner in a mall is approached by the other shop owners about contributing to a new website to market their businesses. Although she is having cash flow problems and sales are down, she gives them $10,000, just to "prove" that her business is doing well and she has the money. Like the hikers, she makes a decision based on ego. As a result, she must borrow money to pay her rent and utilities and cannot order the inventory she needs.

Ego can also get in the way and cause someone not to take action. For example, Andi's coworker comments that Andi has too many spelling errors in the weekly reports she submits to their department supervisor. Andi becomes defensive and merely dismisses the comment. However, the complaint is valid and indicates a problem that Andi could easily correct by taking the time to run her report through spellcheck. By dismissing the criticism, Andi loses the opportunity to make a small change and improve her image on the job. She should take the criticism objectively and determine what action she needs to take.

Practice

How did this student's ego get in the way?

> Rose is taking a course in filmmaking, which he needs to take for his major. Three quarters of his grade are based on a final project, the making of a ten-minute film. Most of the class chose subjects based on their professor's suggestions. However, this student chose to adapt a favorite short story, casting four of his friends in the film. The friends had trouble learning their lines, and it was more difficult to shoot their scenes outdoors than Roger expected. The film was not completed on the due date, and he received a D for the course.

_____

_____

_____

_____

Answer

Never having made a film before, Roger has an exaggerated confidence in his ability, which keeps him from seeing the obvious time limitations of the project. To pass the course, he should have taken the professor's suggestion, like other students, and made a simpler film that could have been finished on time. He could have made the short story adaptation later, on his own time.

In Short

When making decisions, do not ignore your feelings. As you go through the logical steps toward making a choice, acknowledge emotions and, based on the type, decide whether they are appropriate to include in the decision-making process. Even negative feelings, such as bias and stereotyping, need to be recognized so you can consciously exclude them. Acknowledging emotions, rather than letting them take over, or trying to ignore them, will help you improve your critical-thinking skills.

Skill Building Until Next Time

- The next time you attend a sporting event, or watch one on television, pay attention to the fans when the umpire or referee makes a call. Do the fans decide rationally whether the call is fair or not? How do they let their emotions participate in the way they behave?
- Think of a situation that makes you angry, whether it is listening to an opposing political group's speeches, reading a particular columnist in the newspaper, or even going to a sale at your favorite store in which the merchandise was marked up in price before it was marked down. How could you allow your emotions to negatively influence the situation? How could you use them positively?

12 ▶ DEDUCTIVE REASONING

The two operations of our understanding, intuition and deduction, on which alone we have said we must rely in the acquisition of knowledge.

René Descartes, French philosopher, mathematician, scientist (1596–1650)

LESSON SUMMARY

What is deductive reasoning? It's an argument based on two facts, or premises. If both are true, then it should follow that the conclusion of the argument must also be true. In this lesson, you'll learn how these arguments work and don't work. And you'll discover how to use deductive reasoning to construct your own strong arguments

You're exposed to deductive arguments, both good and bad, every day. In a magazine, you read an ad: "Brand X just can't get clothes clean. But with Cleany-Oh, your clothes are sparkly clean!" On TV, you hear a politician: "Higher taxes put people out of work. We need tax cuts. Tax cuts help to create jobs for people!" At a restaurant, you hear a parent say, "If you don't finish your supper, you won't get any dessert."

Understanding how these arguments work and do not work will help you construct strong arguments and make it easier to get your point across. And you'll know when someone else's argument is weak so you're not influenced by faulty reasoning. You'll also be aware if someone is presenting a strong argument that should influence you.

What Is Deduction?

Deduction is the process of drawing a specific conclusion from two things that are known, or general premises. All deductive reasoning includes these three parts:

A. a major premise
B. a minor premise
C. a conclusion

For instance, we know that dogs have four legs, and we know that Fido is a dog. Therefore, since **A** and **B** are true, we can conclude with certainty that Fido has four legs. From this example, you may see that a deductive argument is sound when the premises are true, and the conclusion logically follows from the premises.

Qualities of a Deductive Argument

- Has two premises that provide a guarantee of the truth of the conclusion by providing support for it that is so strong that, if the premises are true, it would be impossible for the conclusion to be false.
- Is described by the terms *valid* and *invalid*; when the premises are correct, and the conclusion that follows is correct, the argument is said to be valid. If either or both premises are incorrect, the argument is invalid.
- Is based on rules, laws, principles, or generalizations, as opposed to inductive arguments (see Lesson 14), whose major premises are based on observations or experiences.

Practice

Which is an example of a deductive argument?

a. There are 25 CDs on the top shelf of my bookcase and 14 on the lower shelf. There are no other CDs in my bookcase. Therefore, there are 39 CDs in my bookcase.
b. Topeka is either in Kansas or Honduras. If Topeka is in Kansas, then Topeka is in North America. If Topeka is in Honduras, then Topeka is in Central America. Therefore, Topeka is in Kansas.
c. No one got an A on yesterday's test. Jimmy wasn't in school yesterday. Jimmy will make up the test today and get an A.
d. All human beings are in favor of world peace. Terrorists don't care about world peace. Terrorists bring about destruction.

Answer

The answer is **a**, because it has two premises and a conclusion that follows logically from them. Choice **b** has three premises and the conclusion does not follow from them. Choices **c** and **d** have conclusions that do not follow the premises.

To be able to detect a deductive argument, and then determine whether or not it is valid, you must be able to figure out what the premises and the conclusion are. Let's look more closely at both of these parts that make up a deductive argument.

Premises

The key to the credibility of a deductive conclusion lies in the premises. Since the conclusion must result from the premises, it is considered invalid if one or both of the premises is proven false. Therefore, the premises must be truthful facts, rules, principles, or generalizations. Just one word can change the premise from fact to fiction, such as the words "all" and "every."

Consider the following example:

> All dogs have brown fur.
> Spot is a dog.
> Spot has brown fur.

The truth is that *some* dogs have brown fur. The first premise is untrue, which makes the conclusion invalid.

Major Premise

A major premise is a statement of general truth dealing with categories rather than individual examples. It relates two terms:

> All women were once girls.
> Athletes are in good shape.
> Professors hold advanced degrees.

The subject of the major premise (women, athletes, professors) is called the *antecedent*; the verb phrase (were once girls, are in good shape, hold advanced degrees) is known as the *consequent*.

Minor Premise

A minor premise is a statement that deals with a specific example of the major premise:

> My mother is a woman.
> Tiger Woods is an athlete.
> Dr. Shiu is a professor.

The minor premise either affirms the major premise, or denies it. When it affirms, part of the minor premise equates with the subject, or antecedent, of the major premise. When it denies, part of the minor premise does not equate with the consequent. For example:

> Children like top 40 music.
> Charles is a child.

In this case, the minor premise (Charles is a child) affirms the major premise by stating that it is something equal to the major premise (child).

> Children like top 40 music.
> Charles does not like top 40 music.

In this case, the minor premise denies the major premise by asserting that something is not the same as the consequent ("does not like" as opposed to "like").

Practice

Which of the following would make the best major premise for a deductive argument? Remember that the two important factors for the major premise are:
1. It relates two terms.
2. It is stated as a generalization, rule, or principle.
   a. No one knows if an asteroid will collide with the Earth.
   b. There are no asteroids.
   c. Those who believe asteroids will hit the Earth have overactive imaginations.
   d. Scientists have proven asteroids will not hit the Earth.

Answer

The best choice is **c** because it relates two terms (asteroids and imaginations), and it is stated as a generalization.

Conclusions

Deductive arguments are those in which the truth of the conclusion is thought to be completely guaranteed and not just made probable by the truth of the premises. So if the argument is valid, the truth of the conclusion is contained within the truth of the premises. But, the conclusion must follow logically from and not go beyond or make assumptions about the premises.

Here is an example of a conclusion that follows the premises:

Banks make money by charging interest.
My bank charges me interest.
My bank makes money.

Note that the conclusion has no additional information, and does not make assumptions or inferences about the premises. It is a valid conclusion.

Here is an example of a conclusion that goes beyond the truth of the premises:

Ernest Hemingway wrote some great books.
Ernest Hemingway wrote *For Whom the Bell Tolls.*
For Whom the Bell Tolls is a great book.

Why is this conclusion invalid? Because the major premise states that some of Hemingway's books are great. The conclusion assumes that *For Whom the Bell Tolls* falls into that group, when there is no evidence in the premises that this is true.

Practice

Change the following invalid conclusion to make it valid.

You have to be 16 years old to get a driver's license. Abby will be 16 years old tomorrow. Therefore, Abby can now buy a car.

Answer

The conclusion should be: Therefore, Abby can now get a driver's license. The deductive argument doesn't say anything about buying a car.

TIP

Did you realize that you use deductive reasoning to prove math facts are accurate?

Two Forms of Deductive Argument

Deductive arguments are expressed in two common ways: syllogisms and conditionals.

Fact or Opinion?

As you learned in Lesson 8, you have to know the difference between a fact and an opinion. A fact is an objective statement that can be proven to be true, such as, "Saturn is one of the planets in our solar system." You can research to prove that Saturn is, indeed, a planet in our solar system. Is that statement always true? If the answer is yes, then it's a fact.

An opinion is a subjective statement based on personal beliefs. For example, "Saturn is the most beautiful planet in the solar system." This is a personal belief and open to debate. Other people might think Venus is the most beautiful planet, or Jupiter. The word *beautiful* is subjective, and tells you this is someone's opinion.

Syllogisms

A syllogism is made up of two premises and a conclusion. The first premise describes a group, A, and a characteristic of that group, B: *All vegetarians do not eat meat*. The second premise places a person or thing, C, either within A or not within B: *Gordon is a vegetarian*. The conclusion states that C is B: *Gordon does not eat meat*.

A negative in a syllogism follows the same form. The word *not* in the second premise signals the negative. *All vegetarians do not eat meat. Gordon is not a vegetarian. Gordon eats meat.*

Here are a few examples of positive and negative syllogisms:

Smart people do not believe in UFOs. (All A are not B)
Lee does not believe in UFOs. (C is not B)
Lee is smart. (C is A)

The greatest jazz artists were all improvisers.
Miles Davis was an improviser.
Miles Davis was a great jazz artist.

Conditionals

A conditional deductive argument expresses the same reasoning in a different way. The first premise states that if something is true of A, then something is true of B: *If you spill the lemonade, then the table will get sticky*. In the second premise, the "if" in A either happens or it doesn't: *You spill the lemonade*, or *You do not spill the lemonade*. The conclusion then states that, as a result, B happens or does not: *The table will get sticky*, or *The table will not get sticky*.

Let's look at some examples:

If you attend Camp HiLow, you will lose weight. (If A, then B)
You attend Camp HiLow. (A)
You lose weight. (B)

If Jason stays after class to speak with his professor, he will miss the bus. (If A then B)
Jason did not stay after class to speak with his professor. (not A)
Jason did not miss the bus. (not B)

If we do not earn the money, we will miss the concert. (If not A, then B)
We earned the money. (A)
We did not miss the concert. (not B)

TIP

Conditional "if . . . then" statements are used when predicting what might happen. **If** *the cold front stalls over our area,* **then** *we're in for another day of possible thunderstorms.*

Practice

State this example as a syllogism and as a conditional deductive argument.

Brian gives a party every time his team wins, so tonight he'll give a party.

Syllogism:

_____

_____

_____

Conditional:

_____

_____

_____

Answer

Syllogism: Every team win means Brian gives a party. The team wins. Brian gives a party.

Conditional: If the team wins, then Brian gives a party. The team wins. Therefore, Brian gives a party.

How Deduction Can Be Misused

People sometimes use deductive arguments incorrectly, deliberately, or by accident. The better you are at spotting such arguments, the less likely you are to accept them as true. Remember, a deductive argument is invalid if either or both of the premises are not true or if the wrong conclusion is reached even though the premises are true. In the next lesson, you learn more about these untruths, called logical fallacies, but for now, here's an example:

> All Americans wear sneakers. (major premise)
> Harold is an American. (minor premise)
> Therefore, Harold wears sneakers. (conclusion)

Since not all Americans wear sneakers, the major premise is false. That makes the conclusion, and therefore the deductive argument itself, invalid.

In this case, the wrong conclusion is reached:

> Many Americans wear sneakers.
> Harold is an American.
> Therefore, Harold wears sneakers.

In Short

Deductive reasoning takes two premises, which may be rules, laws, principles, or generalizations, and forms a conclusion based upon them. In order to be valid, a deductive argument must have premises that are true and a conclusion that logically follows from those premises, without trying to go beyond them. When you understand how these arguments work, you will know how to construct your own strong arguments. You will also avoid being influenced or persuaded by faulty deductive reasoning.

Skill Building Until Next Time

- Find a deductive argument in print. Put it in the form of a diagram, listing the major premise, minor premise, and conclusion. Is it valid? If not, why?
- The next time you need to persuade someone to do something, such as eat at your favorite restaurant instead of theirs or see the movie you prefer, argue for your choice using deductive reasoning.

13 ▶ ERRORS IN DEDUCTIVE REASONING

Logical errors are, I think, of greater practical importance than many people believe; they enable their perpetrators to hold the comfortable opinion on every subject in turn.

Bertrand Russell, British philosopher, mathematician, and historian (1872–1970)

LESSON SUMMARY

An argument with poor reasoning to support its conclusion is called a fallacy. In this lesson, you'll discover the relationship between deductive reasoning and how logic does or doesn't work. And you'll investigate four of the most common logical fallacies people use that make deductive reasoning fall apart.

You learned in Lesson 12 what makes a valid deductive argument—two premises that are true and a conclusion that logically follows from them, without assuming anything not in those premises. A factual error, like a false premise or a conclusion that is not supported by the premises, makes an argument invalid. Moreover, an error in logic can make an argument invalid. This logical error is known as a **fallacy**.

There are a number of logical fallacies that occur in deductive arguments. Sometimes it's hard to recognize such fallacies, but it's important to so you're not misled or persuaded by someone's faulty logic. There are four major logical fallacies:

1. Slippery Slope
2. False Dilemma
3. Circular Reasoning
4. Equivocation

Slippery Slope

As you read in the last lesson, conditionals are premises that use "if . . . then" to lead to a conclusion. Example: *If you oversleep, then you'll miss the bus*. A slippery slope is a conditional that contains a logical fallacy. It doesn't explain how the first event leads to the second. Example: *If you don't pay your electric bill, then you'll never be able to get a loan for a car.*

Slippery slope makes an argument seem more severe; it assumes that one wrong could slide toward something else that is wrong. It leaves out what is "between" the two events, without saying why. In the previous example, there are many possible steps between event A, not paying an electric bill, and event B, not being able to get a car loan. It's true that not paying a bill on time would show up on your credit report, but just one late payment doesn't inescapably lead to having such a bad credit report that you can't get a loan for a car.

Other examples follow. Keep in mind the possible steps between event A and event B in each, and the likelihood, or unlikelihood, that B will ever be a result of A.

- Don't let him help you with that. The next thing you know, he will be running your life.
- You can never give anyone a break. If you do, they will walk all over you.
- This week, you want to stay out past your curfew. If I let you stay out, next week you'll be gone all night!

TIP

Always check an argument for a chain of consequences. When someone says "If this . . . then that," make sure the chains are reasonable.

Practice

Rewrite the following argument to remove the slippery slope fallacy:

> We shouldn't give military aid to other countries. The next thing you know, we will have thousands of troops overseas dying for no good reason.

Answer

Realistic, possible reasons why we should not give military aid to other countries include: it's too dangerous; they will keep asking for more; we shouldn't let our military get spread out too thinly, etc.

False Dilemma

A false dilemma is an argument that presents a limited number of options (usually two), while in reality there are more. In other words, it gives a choice between one or another ("either-or") even though there are other choices that could be made. The false dilemma is commonly seen in black or white terms; it sets up one thing as all good and the other as all bad. Here's an example:

> Stop wasting my time in this store! Either decide you can afford the stereo, or go without music in your room!

This argument contains a logical fallacy because it fails to recognize that there are many other options besides just buying one particular (expensive) stereo and going without music. You could, for instance, buy a less expensive stereo or even a radio. Or, you could borrow a stereo and have music in your room without making a purchase. There are many options beside the two presented as "either-or" in the argument.

Other common false dilemmas include:

Love it or leave it.

Either you're with us, or you're against us.

Get better grades or you will never go to college.

False dilemmas are also common in politics. Many politicians would like you to believe that they, and their party, have all the right answers, and their opponents are not only wrong, but are ruining the country. They set up a choice between all good and all bad. For instance: "Price supports on agricultural production are part of the socialist agenda. My opponent in this race consistently votes for price supports on dairy and tobacco products. It is time to stop electing socialists to Congress. Should you vote for my opponent, who wants to lead our country on the path toward socialism, or should you vote for me and restore democracy?

Practice

Which of the following is NOT a false dilemma?

a. The thing he saw in the sky was either an alien spacecraft or a helicopter.
b. I can't believe my senator voted against the healthcare bill. Either she didn't understand the bill, or she just doesn't care about people less fortunate than herself.
c. The awards are being given out tonight. Either we'll win for best musical this year or we won't.
d. We have to drill for more oil right now or we'll end up with no power for light, heat, cooling, computers, or TV.

Answer

Choice **c** isn't a false dilemma; it's a statement of fact about something that really does have just two possible outcomes: we win or we don't. The other statements each give two options when there are other possibilities.

Circular Reasoning

The conclusion of a valid deductive argument should follow logically from its premises, relying only on the information contained within them. But with the fallacy of circular reasoning, often called *begging the question*, someone assumes as truth the premise he or she is supposed to be proving. In all valid deductions, the conclusion—what someone is trying to prove—follows two premises; in an invalid circular-reasoning argument, the conclusion follows a single premise. In other words, a premise that's supposed to prove the truth of the conclusion is just the conclusion restated with a slight variation.

When a premise is left out, there is no argument. The person making the claim is simply telling you to believe that what he or she is telling you is true.

Examples

1. "I told you to clean your room!" "Why?" "Because I said so!"
2. "Why do you think the Yankees are the best team in baseball?" "Because they are."

How could these examples go from being invalid to valid, logical arguments? They need a second premise that supports, or gives reason for, the conclusion. Example 1 might add: "Your room is so messy that you can't find anything in it," or, "All of your laundry is on the floor, and it won't get washed until you clean it up and put it in the washer." Example 2 could add: "They have won the World Series 27 times," or, "They are the only team to sweep the World Series ten times."

TIP

Identify the most important words and phrases in an argument and ask yourself if they have more than one meaning. If they do, be sure you know which is the correct meaning for the situation.

Practice

Which of the following does not beg the question?

a. I like the Brewers because they're my favorite team.

b. Ghosts exist because I saw something once that could only have been a ghost.

c. The Seafood Shack is the best restaurant in town because it's so much better than all the others.

d. They signed Bruce Springsteen to headline the concert because he's a rock legend and a huge star.

Answer

Choice **d** does not beg the question. It gives two reasons why Springsteen was signed. It would have been an example of circular reasoning if it said: "They signed Bruce Springsteen to headline the concert because he's a concert headliner."

Equivocation

Sometimes the fallacy of equivocation can be difficult to spot because both premises seem to be true, and often the conclusion seems to follow them. However, the meaning of the entire argument becomes invalid because either (1) a word is used twice, each time with a different meaning, or (2) a word with several meanings is used just once but gives the statement an ambiguous meaning. The ambiguity isn't due to grammar, but to the distinct meanings of the words.

> *Examples*
>
> My history professor said everyone who wrote a term paper favoring the separatists in the Philippines is sick. I guess if I'm sick, I can skip class today.

The word "sick" is used in the argument twice, each with a different meaning. The professor meant emotionally troubled, and the student thought he meant physically ill.

> Hot dogs are better than nothing. Nothing is better than steak. Therefore, hot dogs are better than steak.

It is not hard to spot the logical fallacy here: The conclusion is obviously wrong although the premises are both true. There is an equivocation in the meaning of the word "nothing"; in the first premise, it means "not a thing," and in the second premise, it means "no other possible thing." Using a critical word with two different meanings makes the argument invalid.

The second way an argument becomes invalid due to equivocation is when a word, used only once, has several meanings. For example, "Save soap and waste paper." Here, the word *waste* could mean either the noun "garbage," or the verb "to use thoughtlessly." The equivocation of the word *waste* makes the meaning of the sentence unclear.

Equivocation can be confusing because it begins with truthful or reasonable premises, which you can agree with. Then, the meaning of a critical word is changed and an illogical or faulty conclusion is drawn. If you follow the argument, you could fall into the trap of agreeing with something you would never have otherwise accepted. The best way to handle this fallacy is to get information. Ask for clear definitions of any critical terms that could be used in different ways.

Practice

Which word in each example is the equivocation?

1. A feather is light. Something light can't be dark. So a feather can't be dark.
2. It's just natural to want to save our natural resources.
3. Mark's parents told him to do what's right. He has the right to drop out of school at age 18. Therefore, 17-year-old Mark should drop out of school on his next birthday.
4. Branches have leaves. A bank has branches, so bank branches must have leaves.

Answer

1. light 2. natural 3. right 4. branches

In Short

Not all deductive reasoning is reasonable. It may be flawed factually, meaning all or part of it is untrue. Or it may be flawed logically, and contain a fallacy. It is important to recognize logical fallacies so they do not persuade or mislead you. Some of the most common of these fallacies are slippery slope, false dilemma, circular reasoning, and equivocation.

TIP

People who use logical fallacies imply that we're ignorant and incapable of seeing through their deception. Prove them wrong! Learn to spot each kind.

Skill Building Until Next Time

- Find a newspaper or magazine article that contains quotes from one or more politicians. Do any of them use logical fallacies in their arguments? If so, which fallacies, and how?
- Think of an extravagant purchase you would like to make. Devise two arguments for buying the item, using both false dilemma and circular reasoning fallacies.

14 ▶ INDUCTIVE REASONING

The deductive method is the mode of using knowledge, and the inductive method the mode of acquiring it.

Henry Mayhew, English journalist and playwright (1812–1887)

LESSON SUMMARY

You just investigated deductive arguments, the kind built on laws and principles, that move from generalizations to specific conclusions. Now it's time to look at the other kind of reasoning: inductive arguments. They're built on common sense and/or past experience, moving from specific facts to general conclusions. In this lesson, you'll learn to recognize and construct arguments that use inductive reasoning.

Induction is the process of reasoning from specific facts or occurrences to general principles, theories, and rules. Used in scientific hypotheses, inductive thinking uses two conditional premises that support a probable truth in the conclusion: If A is true **and** B is true, then C is probably true.

In inductive reasoning, we determine or measure what's probable or improbable by using two things:

1. past experience
2. common sense

Past experience lets you predict what you think might happen the next time there's a similar situation. For example, "For the past three weeks, Bob's been a half-hour late for work. Today, he'll probably be late again."

Common sense allows you to make an inference, or "smart guess," based on known facts or premises. For example, "They must have five people on their team. I'm one of the best of the seven players at the tryouts. So it's likely I'll be picked for the team."

You learned that in deductive reasoning, a conclusion had to be true if the premises were true. But with inductive reasoning, the premises are good reasons for thinking the conclusion is correct, but there's always a possibility that, although the premises are true, the conclusion will be false. In other words, there's no automatic, logical link between premises and conclusion. So inductive reasoning is more likely than deductive reasoning to fail and produce fallacies, like a hasty conclusion fallacy (see Lesson 15 for more on these fallacies).

Even with its flaws, inductive reasoning is the type of reasoning we use most often. The cell theory, one of the basics of modern biology, is a product of inductive reasoning: *Every organism observed is made up of cells; therefore, it is most likely that all living things are made up of cells.*

There are two forms of inductive arguments: comparative arguments match one thing, event, or idea up against another to see if they're similar; causal arguments try to determine cause from effect.

TIP

In science, inductive reasoning is essential for discovering relationships as you create logical hypotheses and theories.

Practice

Choose the best conclusion for this argument: The other people who live in my apartment building

a. like Thai food, so I should, too.

b. do their laundry on Tuesdays, so I should, too.

c. don't seem to like the new superintendent, so I won't either.

d. pay their rent on the first of the month, so I will, too.

Answer

The correct answer is choice **d**. From past experience, you may know that rent is due on the first of the month, and common sense tells you that if other renters pay on the first, that must be when rent is due.

Comparison Arguments

Inductive arguments compare one event, idea, or thing with another to conclude if they are similar enough to make a generalization or inference about them. The most important characteristic of the argument is that the two events being compared must be similar.

Example

Rebekah says, "Whenever I use bread flour to make my pizza, the crust turns out perfectly. So, every time I use bread flour, I will have a perfect pizza crust." (A leads to B many times, so A will lead to B every time.)

Rebekah is comparing one thing (use of bread flour for pizza crust) with another (bread flour producing a perfect crust). The two things have one similarity: bread flour. The inductive argument produces a generalization: Any time she uses bread flour to make pizza dough, she'll get perfect pizza crust.

The strength of this, as well as all other, comparative inductive arguments depends on how similar the two things are. In fact, when an inductive argument fails, it is most often because the events were not really similar enough to make a comparison. Rebekah takes for granted that "every time" in the future, she will make pizza exactly as she did during each of the observed times. If that is true, her conclusion is probably true.

But what if every observed time Rebekah used the bread flour, she also used fresh yeast? If she makes a pizza in the future with packaged yeast, she will not get a perfect crust. The events will be dissimilar, so the conclusion will not hold. The second premise of any inductive argument should ideally state that there is no significant difference between the two sets of events/ideas/things. The second premise of Rebekah's argument could say "Every crust will be perfect, because there will be no key difference between my future crust making and my previous crust making." Keeping such a disclaimer in mind is important, because this is where many inductive arguments are weakest.

Practice

What conclusion could you make from the following inductive argument?

> We have read over one hundred pages of her poetry manuscript. So far, the poems about nature are strong and finely crafted, and those about love and relationships are loose and even sometimes sloppy. So in the next hundred pages, we can expect to find . . .

Answer

You can conclude "that her love poetry is loose and sometimes sloppy, and her nature poetry is finely crafted."

Practice

Which is NOT an example of a comparison argument?

a. Last week I washed my clothes on Monday and didn't run out of clean clothes all week. This Monday I'm going to wash my clothes so I don't run out of clean clothes this week.
b. For the last two weeks, I've returned my library books on time and didn't have to pay late fees. This week I'm going to return my books on time, too, so I don't get charged late fees.
c. Jim said he had the best, tastiest, juiciest burger at Carlo's restaurant yesterday. Today, he says he's going to eat at Frank's Fast Food.
d. The past five Januarys, the department stores had white sales of towels and linens. This January, they'll probably have sales on towels and linens, too.

Answer

The correct answer is choice c. The other answer choices all show a similarity between one event and the other.

Causal Arguments

The previously mentioned inductive arguments relied on the similarities between two things. Causal arguments rely instead on finding a key difference to determine the probable cause of an effect. Why is it important to determine cause? If you believe that one thing is the reason (cause) that another thing happened (effect), you may want to either (1) reproduce that relationship and cause that effect again, or (2) prevent the relationship from happening again.

For example, every time you study hard for a test, you get a good grade. If you want to keep getting good grades, you want to know if there is a link between studying hard and getting good grades. When you can determine cause and effect, you can repeat the effect. In this case, that means figuring out that the studying really does result in good grades. To continue to get good grades, therefore, you need to continue to study hard for every test.

On the other hand, what if you have been studying and getting good grades and there is a test coming up? You are busy with other things and don't study for it. You get a D on the test. The argument goes like this:

Every time I have a test coming up, I study for it and get good grades. This time, I didn't study, and I got a D. If I don't want to get more Ds in the future, I'll prevent the unwanted result by preventing the cause. In this case, the key difference means if you don't want bad grades, you must study. Remember that in order to determine cause, an argument must be formed that looks for a key difference between two otherwise similar events.

Here is another example:

Jen had a stomachache on Thursday and is trying to figure out why. Every morning for breakfast she eats bran cereal with skim milk and a banana. But on Thursday she was out of milk and had toast for breakfast instead. By midmorning, she had a painful stomachache. She picked up milk on the way home from work and had her usual breakfast on Friday. The stomachache did not occur on Friday. Nothing else in her routine was out of the ordinary.

What caused the stomachache? Chances are it was the breakfast she ate on Thursday. It's the key difference. Every morning when she eats her regular breakfast, she feels fine, but gets a stomachache the one morning she eats only toast instead. Perhaps she was hungry, having had less to eat. However, not all examples are this easy to spot. It may require an inference based on information in the argument.

Real-life situations can get complicated. Our lives and the world around us are affected by thousands of details, making the finding of one key difference difficult. That said, if there is a strong likelihood of causation and there are no other obvious causes, you can make a convincing causal argument. But you need to have the following:

- **The effect must occur after the cause.** This sounds like common sense, but there are many arguments that place the effect before the cause.
Example
You are blamed for a computer problem at work. However, you did not use the computer until after the problem was detected. The argument against you has no strength.
- **You need more than just a strong correlation to prove causation.** Coincidence can often explain what might first appear to be cause and effect.
Example
Every time you wear your blue sweater, your team wins the game. Can you determine that if you always wear the sweater, your team will always win? The answer is no, because there is no causation. Nothing about your wearing the sweater could have caused a certain outcome in a game.

TIP

When you play cards or a game like chess, you use inductive reasoning to recognize patterns, follow known theories, and form new hypotheses as needed.

Practice
Look for causation in the following scenario.

Yesterday, I pulled out of a diagonal parking spot and was starting to turn my wheel and move forward, when another car backed out of a spot behind me. She drove right into me, smashing my left rear door with the corner of her bumper. The other driver told the police officer that I hit her. But he agreed with me that it was her fault, and wrote down why on the police report.

What did the police officer write? Chose all that could apply.

a. Drivers must wait their turn if another car is already pulling out of a parking space behind them. It is clear that the first car was already out of her space when she was hit on her door.

b. It is impossible to hit the corner of someone's bumper with your rear door when backing out of a parking spot. It is possible to hit the rear door of someone's car with the corner of your bumper.

c. Speeding in parking lots is prohibited by law.

d. The other driver must not have been looking in her rearview mirror, or she would not have backed into the other car.

Answer

The probable causes of the car accident are **a**, **b**, and **d**. While speeding in parking lots is never a good idea, it was not a cause of this accident.

In Short

Inductive reasoning uses specific information that has been observed or experienced, and draws general conclusions about it. To make those conclusions, it relies on either (or both) past experience and common sense. Because the conclusions can only state what is likely or probable, there is a greater chance of error with inductive reasoning as opposed to deductive reasoning. In the next lesson, you will learn about specific ways in which inductive reasoning goes wrong.

Skill Building Until Next Time

You are always drawing conclusions from your observations. Pay attention to this inductive reasoning and evaluate your skills. Are you using common sense and/or past experience? Have you noticed a key difference, or compared two similar events? Become a better user of inductive reasoning by being aware of when and how you use it.

15 ▶ ERRORS IN INDUCTIVE REASONING

All generalizations are false, including this one.
Mark Twain, American author and humorist (1835–1910)

LESSON SUMMARY
As with deductive reasoning, an inductive argument that has poor reasoning to support its conclusion is a fallacy. An inductive fallacy has either two premises that don't support its conclusion, or a conclusion that doesn't fit the premises. In this lesson, you'll learn how to spot some common logical fallacies so you're not taken in by their faulty logic.

The conclusion drawn in an inductive argument is only as good as the quantity and quality of its premises. There are many ways to create a strong inductive argument, and just as many ways to create a weak one. It's important to understand the different logical fallacies that can make an argument weak, so you'll know one when you see or hear them, and avoid using them yourself.

Chicken-and-Egg Fallacy

"Which came first, the chicken or the egg?" That age-old question is used to classify problems for which there are no easy answers. What does that have to do with inductive arguments? If you're creating a logical argument, using two events, you can't take it for granted that because the two things regularly happen together, one causes the other. That's the chicken-and-egg fallacy. It follows this general form:

1. A and B regularly occur together.
2. Therefore, A is the cause of B.

This fallacy assumes that one event must cause another just because the events occur together. The assumption is based on inadequate justification; there is not enough evidence to draw the causal conclusion.

A common example of chicken-and-egg fallacy is the relationship between TV/movie violence and real-life violent behavior. Many people believe that a person's violent behavior is the result of watching TV/ movie violence. Other people contend that if someone is a violent person, he or she will create, watch, and enjoy violent programming. So, does TV/movie violence cause real-life violence, or vice versa? Or is there no causal relationship between the two? The simple fact is that some people are violent, and some entertaining TV shows and movies contain violence. But there is not enough evidence to assert a connection, since many people watch violent TV shows/movies and never become violent themselves.

How can you avoid falling into the chicken-and-egg fallacy? Since it means drawing a conclusion without enough evidence presented to show any cause-and-effect relationship, you can avoid it by paying careful attention to the sequence of events. If A happens after B, A can't possibly cause B. Ask yourself if there's anything else that could have been the cause. Think about the evidence presented. Is it enough to draw the conclusion?

Examples
- Many smokers have lung cancer. Lung cancer causes people to smoke.
- You can't get a job unless you have experience. You can't get experience unless someone gives you a job!
- Last night I had a fever. This morning, I have a cold and a fever. The fever caused the cold.

Practice
Which of the following is NOT a chicken-and-egg fallacy?
  a. Jay Leno is famous. He is also on television frequently. Jay Leno is famous because he is on television frequently.
  b. I didn't wash dishes all week. My dirty dishes started to grow mold. If I don't want mold growing on my dishes, I should wash them.
  c. My boss really liked the work I did on my latest project. I didn't work as hard on the project as I usually do. In order to make my boss happy, I shouldn't work as hard as I usually do.
  d. Your grades went down this semester. You joined a study group this semester. Your grades went down because you joined the study group.

Answer
Choice **b** is not a chicken-and-egg fallacy; it is a logical inductive argument. Choices **a**, **c**, and **d** are all examples of chicken and egg arguments. There is not enough information in any of the premises to be able to draw their conclusions. Either there is a common cause of both A and B, or a reversal (B caused A, and not the other way around).

Hasty Generalization

In this fallacy, there's not enough data or cases to warrant a generalization, For example, a waitress complains, "Those Southerners left me a lousy tip. All Southerners are cheap!" She has made a generalization about tens of millions of people based on an experience with a few of them. A hasty generalization like hers takes this form:

1. A very small sample A is taken from population B.
2. Generalization C is made about population B based on sample A.

There are two common reasons for hasty generalizations. One is because of bias or prejudice. For instance, a sexist person could conclude that all women are bad drivers because he had an accident with one. Hasty generalizations are also often made because of negligence or laziness. It is not always easy to get a large enough sample to draw a reasonable conclusion. But if you can't get the right sample, do not make the generalization. Better yet, make an attempt to add to your sample size. Improve your argument with better evidence.

How do you know when your sample is large enough? There is no one rule that applies to every type of sample, so you will need to use the "practicality and reasonability" test. What is the largest sample you can gather that makes sense, practically? Will it be large enough so that you can reasonably make a generalization about it? Reread the section on statistics in Lesson 10 to refresh your memory about the problems that can occur when taking a sample, and how those problems can be recognized and/or avoided.

Try to avoid jumping to conclusions, and learn to spot when others have done so in their arguments. If a generalization is the result of prior opinions about people in question, the bias needs to be removed and the generalization rethought, based on real information. You also need to take the time to get a large enough sample so that a generalization drawn from that sample makes sense. To generalize about a large group of people, you need to find out about many more of them than when generalizing about a very small group.

Examples

- I asked eight of my coworkers what they thought of the new manufacturing rules, and they all thought they are a bad idea. The new rules are generally unpopular.

- That new police drama is a really well done show. All police dramas are great shows.
- Omar threw the ball from left field to the second baseman, and he made an incredible double play. Whenever Omar gets the ball, he should throw it to the second baseman.

Practice

How could this argument be changed from a hasty generalization to a strong inductive argument?

Sven is visiting the United States on vacation. He goes into a bank to exchange money, and is surprised to find he is the only one in line. That night, he e-mails his family, "Banking is so much faster in America. You can go into any bank and never have to wait in line."

_____

_____

_____

_____

Answer

Sven based his conclusion, "Banking is faster in America," on one experience at one bank. In order for his hasty generalization to become a strong argument, he'd have to visit many more banks to determine if they also have short lines and brief wait times before coming to the same conclusion.

TIP

You can avoid erroneous generalizations by being specific. People should know exactly what your message is.

Composition

This fallacy occurs when the qualities of the parts of a whole are assumed to also be the qualities of the whole. It is a fallacy because there is no justification for making this assumption. For example, someone might argue that because every individual part of a large machine is lightweight, the machine itself is lightweight.

This argument is fallacious; you cannot conclude that because the parts of a whole have (or lack) certain qualities, the whole that they are parts of has those qualities. Let's look at another example. A girl's mother tells her, "You love meatloaf, applesauce, ice cream, and pickles. So, you will love what we're having for dinner tonight! I made a meatloaf, applesauce, ice cream, and pickle casserole." This is an example of the fallacy of composition because, while the girl loves all of those foods individually, one cannot reasonably conclude that she will love them when they are put together as a casserole (a whole made of the likeable parts is not necessarily likeable).

Sometimes an argument that states the properties of the parts are also the properties of the whole can be a strong one. For example, if every piece of a table is wood, there's no fallacy in the conclusion that the whole table is wood. To determine whether a statement is fallacious or not, you need to determine if there's a justification for the inference from parts to whole.

Practice

Which is NOT a composition fallacy?
  a. The special effects in that movie were excellent, so the whole movie must be excellent.
  b. A spider's body is made up of atoms, which are invisible to the naked eye. Therefore, a spider is invisible to the naked eye.
  c. This sauce is a mixture of six kinds of cheese. Therefore, the sauce is a cheese sauce.
  d. A cheetah eats more food per day than a human does. Therefore, cheetahs, as a species, eat more food than all the humans on Earth do.

Answer

Choice **c** is not a fallacy. If the main parts (ingredients) in the sauce are cheese, then the whole is a cheese sauce.

Post Hoc, Ergo Propter Hoc

When you read about the chicken-and-egg fallacy earlier in this lesson, you noted that just because one event precedes another doesn't mean that the first caused the second. To assume it does is another illogical fallacy known as *post hoc, ergo propter hoc,* Latin for, "after this, therefore because of this." Often shortened to just *post hoc* and sometimes referred to as false cause, this fallacy follows the pattern:

  1. Event A precedes event B.
  2. Event A caused event B.

But to make a strong causal argument, you must account for all relevant details. For example, every time Ahmed tries to open a video program on his computer, it crashes. He concludes that the program is causing the computer to crash. However, computers are complex machines, and there could be many other causes for the crashes. The fact that the opening of one program always precedes the crash is a good possibility for cause, but it cannot be maintained as the one and only cause until a stronger link is made. To avoid the *post hoc* fallacy, he would need to show that all of the many other possibilities for the cause of the crashing have been evaluated and proven to be irrelevant.

Superstitions are another example of *post hoc* fallacies. Some superstitions are widely held, such as "if you break a mirror, you will have seven years of bad luck." Others are more personal, such as the wearing of a lucky article of clothing. However, all of them are *post hoc* fallacies because they do not account for the many other possible causes of the effect. Bad luck could happen to someone who breaks a mirror, but bad things also happen to those who do not. In these cases of superstitions, the real cause is usually coincidence.

How can you strengthen an argument and keep it from becoming an example of the *post hoc* fallacy? First, show that the effect would not occur if the cause did not occur. For example, if I don't strike the match, it will not catch on fire. Second, be certain there is no other cause that could result in the effect. Are there any sources of flame near the match? Do matches spontaneously catch fire? Is there anything else that could cause it to catch fire? If the answer is no, then there is no *post hoc* fallacy.

Examples

- I took three echinacea tablets every day when my cold started. Within a week, my cold was gone, thanks to the echinacea.
- I wanted to do well on the test, so I used my lucky pen. It worked again! I got an A.
- Last night I had a dream that there was a car accident in my town. When I read the paper this morning, I found out a car accident did happen last night. My dreams predict the future.

Practice

Which is an example of a *post hoc* fallacy?

a. I wanted to take part in the 5K race. I trained every day and ran a good race. If I want to run the race next year, I need to train for it.
b. Diane decided to knit a sweater for her dad, so she bought yarn in his favorite color and followed the knitting instructions exactly. Her dad loved it.
c. Zoe wore a black velvet costume the day she won her first figure skating championship. She decided to wear black velvet again today so she would win. It worked!
d. Vibrating sound waves can actually shatter glass. The opera singer hit a very high note and a glass broke.

Answer

Choice **c** is a *post hoc* fallacy because it claims that Zoe's dress caused her to win a skating competition. Obviously, in any sport, skill, training, endurance, or a lack of those things play a big part in winning or losing. Also, Zoe's opponents' performances came into play. How a skater looks may be important, but a costume alone wouldn't change how a skater was judged.

TIP

If you say that A causes B, have something more to say about **how** other than just that it came first! You might want to use data and statistics to make your point.

In Short

Inductive reasoning is used all the time to make generalizations from specifics. But it can be misused to create arguments for things such as racial prejudice and superstitions. These weak arguments involve fallacies such as hasty conclusions, chicken and egg, and composition (making a conclusion about a whole based on the qualities of its parts). Learning how to recognize such faulty reasoning will help you to avoid being tricked by it, and also help you avoid making such mistakes in your arguments.

Skill Building Until Next Time

- Read the science section of your newspaper or a science article in a magazine and find an example of inductive reasoning. Check for fallacies. If none exist, come up with a way to apply one of the fallacies in this lesson to the example.
- Remember that in order to determine cause, you must have enough evidence to support the conclusion. The next time you are blamed for something or hear someone blaming another person, think about this: Do they have strong premises on which to base their conclusion? Who or what could have been the real cause?

16 ▶ DISTRACTING TECHNIQUES

The first point of wisdom is to discern that which is false; the second, to know that which is true.

Lactantius, North-African author and
rhetoric teacher (c. 250–325 B.C.E.)

LESSON SUMMARY

You read and hear arguments every day, in magazine and newspaper ads and articles, and in ads and political speeches on TV. Some arguments are logically sound, but as you discovered in Lessons 13 and 15, some contain logical fallacies that make them invalid. Some fallacies might show up accidentally, but in this lesson, you'll learn about red herring, *ad hominem*, and straw man fallacies, the kind that deliberately aim to distract you from the real issue in an argument.

After you've watched a debate between political candidates, do you ever wonder "what just happened"? Many people do—so many that right after a debate, TV station pundits have to rehash what was said so the average person can understand the debate! Debates should be about the real issues facing voters, and how each candidate plans to solve them. Instead, candidates' remarks are often filled with distracting techniques designed to shift focus from the real issues and put opponents on the defensive.

Three often-used focus-shifting techniques are **red herring**, *ad hominem*, and **straw man** fallacies. Although relatively easy to spot, these logical fallacies can be challenging to deflect—if one is aimed at you, it's critical to know how it works so you can refocus your attention on the real issue.

Red Herring

This may seem like an odd name for a common logical fallacy. The term comes from an archaic practice of using strong-smelling fish to distract hounds from a fainter scent during their training. A red herring fallacy is simply any unrelated topic brought into an argument to divert attention from the subject at hand. A person on the defensive end of an argument changes the subject from one that he or she feels uncomfortable with to one he or she knows more about. A red herring fallacy looks like this:

1. There is discussion of issue A.
2. There is an introduction of issue B (irrelevant to issue A, but pretending to be relevant).
3. Issue A is forgotten and issue B becomes the focal point.

Example

"Nuclear power is a necessity, even though it has the potential to be dangerous. You know what is really dangerous, though? Bathtubs. More people die in accidents in their bathtubs every year than you can imagine."

Where's the red herring? Quite simply, the speaker changed the subject from issue A, the danger of nuclear power, to the irrelevant issue B, bathtub dangers. Then, the speaker goes on with a statistic about issue B, and issue A is forgotten!

Red herrings work well if the distracter is something many people will agree with or seems to be closely related to the original issue. For example, someone might throw in a comment about how no one likes paying higher taxes or working longer hours. Who would disagree? Here's an example:

"Okay, since the new boss came on board, he seems to be getting the job done, but how about the longer hours? Are you happy about your new work schedule? You have less time with your family, and you're not making any more money than before!"

The speaker diverted attention from the new boss doing a good job to the topic of working more hours and not being paid more. The red herring might have worked, as listeners probably would be more interested in evaluating their own circumstances rather than hear how great the boss is.

Practice

What's the red herring in this argument? How might the argument continue without a red herring?

> "I shouldn't have to pay this parking ticket! The police should be doing what we pay them to do and get the muggers and other dangerous criminals off the street, instead of picking on an honest taxpayer like me!"

_____

_____

_____

_____

_____

Answer

The argument is supposed to be about paying a parking ticket, but the red herring shifts it to blaming local police for not doing their jobs. The argument could be effective by giving reasons for not deserving the fine, such as "I was about to put money in the meter as the officer was writing the ticket," "I parked for just a minute to take my sister into the hospital emergency room," or "The sign that posted hours for parking had fallen off, so I didn't know you couldn't park here on Thursdays."

> ### TIP
>
> To assure that you don't have any red herrings in your arguments, write your premises and conclusion in outline form. Make sure you can explain how each premise supports the conclusion.

Ad Hominem

Another common distraction fallacy is *ad hominem* (Latin for "against the person"). It refers to an attack on the person making an argument rather than on the argument itself. Instead of arguing against a topic, a speaker rejects that topic and throws in some unrelated fact about the opponent. By shifting the focus to the person, the original topic is forgotten, and the person under attack is forced to go on the defensive.

If you're not thinking critically, you might be persuaded by an *ad hominem* argument, especially if you agree with what is being said about the person. For example, picture a celebrity athlete doing a car ad on TV, talking about the car's great gas mileage and service record. Suddenly your friend announces, "Who'd believe anything that jerk says? He can't throw a ball to save his life!" Now, imagine that you actually agree about the athlete's lousy ability. That might make it tougher for you to spot your friend's illogical distracter. The athlete's ability isn't important here; what he's saying about the car is.

Ad hominem arguments are made in three ways, all of which attempt to direct attention away from the argument being made and onto the person making it.

1. **Abusive:** an attack on the character or personal traits of the opposition. These attacks can work well if the person being attacked defends himself or herself and gets distracted from the issue at hand.

Examples
- Your professor may have given a great lecture on the expansion of the universe, but the word around campus is that he is an unfair grader.
- She is giving you stock tips? I would not listen to her advice; just look at that horrible outfit she is wearing.

2. **Circumstantial:** irrelevant personal circumstances of the person making the argument are used to distract attention from the argument and used as evidence against it. This often includes phrases like "that is what you would expect him to do."

Examples
- Representative Murray's speech about getting rid of the estate tax is ridiculous. Obviously, he is going to benefit from it!
- Don't pay attention to what the power company is saying; they get their funding from the nuclear energy industry.

3. ***Tu quoque:*** argues that the argument is irrelevant, because the person presenting it does not practice what he or she preaches or is in some other way inconsistent. Like the abusive *ad hominem* fallacy, *tu quoque* can be effective because the person being attacked often drops his or her argument in order to defend him- or herself.

Examples
- Why should I listen to you? You tell me to stop buying lottery tickets, but you go to Atlantic City and gamble away thousands in just one night!
- His speech about the new prison reforms was pretty convincing, if you can forget that he is an ex-con.

Straw Man

This fallacy got its name from an old question, "Which is easier to fight, a real man or one made of straw?" If given the choice, most people pick the straw man, because it's so weak that it could be toppled by a breeze. Thus straw man fallacies deliberately distort an opponent's view on an issue in order to create an argument that's easier to win . . . it'll be a breeze!

The weaker position, or straw man, is usually an exaggerated or distorted version of the real position. Suppose a couple is having an argument about money. The wife is upset because her husband has been charging expensive items on their charge card. "You have to be more careful with our money," she tells him. Her husband retorts, "Why should I listen to you? You don't want me to spend a penny!"

Where is the straw man? Instead of acknowledging the issue his wife brought up, the husband distorts it by exaggeration. By changing his wife's claim to something ridiculous, he dismisses it. She didn't say he should spend nothing (an extreme view), but just that he should be more careful.

Note that the straw man fallacy attacks a position that isn't actually held by the opponent. A conclusion is drawn that ignores the real issue, so the person defending him- or herself has to bypass the real issue, too. In the previous scenario, the husband dismisses his wife's real argument—that he should be more careful with their money—by creating a new and unreasonable position for his wife to argue against. She's forced to counter his argument with something like, "I never said you shouldn't spend *any* money. Of course you should, you helped to earn it!" He never takes responsibility for the original issue.

It's difficult to defend against a straw man fallacy because you're forced to refute an extreme position you weren't taking in the first place, while trying to bring the focus back to the original argument. For example, it's a straw man fallacy to say that all Republicans care only for the rich or all Democrats want to create and

---

TIP

It's important to know the difference between an insult and an *ad hominem* fallacy. An insult just tries to belittle someone; an *ad hominem* fallacy tries to attack an argument based on the person making it.

Practice

Identify each *ad hominem* fallacy as (A) abusive, (C) circumstantial, or (TQ) *tu quoque*.

___ 1. How can you believe that study on smoking? The tobacco industry funded it!

___ 2. In the last vote, you went against the gun control bill, saying it did not go far enough. Now you are voting for it, so I guess you were wrong about it not going far enough.

___ 3. I know she won't come with us to the gangster movie. She is not a guy—she only likes chick flicks.

___ 4. How can you believe that guy's views on environmental policy? Look at him—he is such a weirdo.

Answer

1. **C**, Circumstantial; the tobacco industry could gain from the study.

2. **TQ**, *Tu quoque*; it says the person's argument against the bill was wrong because she changed her position on it.

3. **C**, Circumstantial; her views on the movie are not important—she is female, so what do you expect?

4. **A**, Abusive; the policy views have nothing to do with how someone looks.

defend a welfare state. Imagine a Democrat who does support welfare faced with such a remark. First, the person would have to try to show that the remark is excessive, then try to bring the discussion back to a reasonable view of the benefits of welfare.

Examples

- We are all being asked to take a pay cut until the economy picks up. I can't believe they expect us to live on nothing!
- You want me to vacuum the family room? I just cleaned it up two days ago. I can't spend my life cleaning, you know.
- Congress is voting on reducing military spending. What do they want us to do, defend ourselves with paper airplanes?

Practice

Which is NOT an example of a straw man?

a. My math teacher assigns too much work. She expects us to do homework all night.
b. Can you believe they want to end the tax cuts? Tomorrow, they will be asking us to send back our tax refund checks!
c. The Yankees are in the playoffs again. It is all about money. Give me millions of dollars, and I could put a winning team together, too.
d. Why can't we all get along? I know we have different opinions on this issue, but it is not like we are at war.

Answer

Choice **d** is not an example of a straw man. Choices **a**, **b**, and **c** are all straw men because they distract from the real issues by turning them into exaggerations, distortions, and extremes.

In Short

Why would someone want to use a distracting technique? Perhaps they are faced with an argument they feel they can't win or they are uncomfortable discussing a certain topic. Whatever the reason, techniques such as red herrings, *ad hominem* attacks, and straw man are commonly used, not only by politicians and pundits, but by schoolchildren, business people, and friends. Learning how these fallacies work will hone your critical-thinking skills and help keep you from falling victim to their faulty reasoning.

Skill Building Until Next Time

- Think of an issue you feel strongly about. Now, come up with an argument against that issue that includes an *ad hominem* attack. Make it as effective as you can. How would you argue against it, without getting defensive?
- Listen for a few minutes to a radio program known for its controversial host. As the host discusses his or her opponents, note how many times straw man is used. How extreme are these arguments, and what are the real issues they are distracting the audience from?

17 ▶ MAKING JUDGMENT CALLS

You can use all the quantitative data you can get, but you still have to distrust it and use your own intelligence and judgment.

Alvin Toffler, American writer and futurist (1928–)

LESSON SUMMARY

Sometimes you come across a problem for which there is no right or wrong answer. So how do you figure out what to do? In this lesson, you'll learn how to make judgments, or personal decisions, when those kinds of problems present themselves.

Most of the critical-thinking skills you've explored so far in this book have been about gathering facts, and then making decisions based on those facts. Although doing so is not always easy, the process from problem to solution is clear cut: identify and understand the situation, learn everything you can about it and any possible solutions available, and then choose the best one. However, sometimes you can't find enough information to make a decision because it doesn't exist, so there is no right answer. At times like that, you have to make a judgment call.

What Is a Judgment Call?

Judgment calls are important decisions made all the time, about things like what stock to buy, when to perform a surgery, and whether a potentially game-winning basketball shot made it through the hoop before the buzzer. But these decisions do have a number of things in common. For instance:

- the stakes are high
- the information you need is incomplete or ambiguous
- knowledgeable people disagree about them
- there are often ethical dilemmas and/or conflicting values involved

How can you make a judgment call with so much uncertainty surrounding the issue? Remember that these types of decisions, however difficult, are made all the time. Each one has an outcome that is both subjective and debatable. That is, judgment calls are not made purely on facts because the facts are not completely available. They are debatable because another person, who knows as much as you do about the decision and the situation surrounding it, could come up with a strong argument as to why your decision might be wrong (or another option is right). Accepting the nature of judgment calls before you make then can help take some of the stress out of the decision-making process.

Preparing to Make a Judgment Call

If you can't gather enough information to make a decision, is there any way to prepare for making a judgment call? The answer is yes. Some facts may be unclear, so it's debatable which to include and which to exclude, but arming yourself with as much information as possible is an important step in preparing to make a judgment call.

Example
A food pantry opens in a small town to provide free food and household items to needy people. After a few months, the number of people visiting the pantry doubles as word spreads to surrounding communities. Most of the new visitors come from a city ten miles away that has its own food pantry. The people who run the small-town pantry discover that some of the new visitors are taking the food back to the city and selling it. Should the committee ignore this and continue to provide food for anyone who comes in? Should the pantry be limited to only those who live in the town? Should the committee close the pantry and discontinue its mission?

This needs a real-life judgment call. Imagine you're on the committee. What would you do?

The first step is to gather information, identify all available options, and try to determine on what you need to base your decision. Do most people who visit the food pantry have an actual need? If the food pantry closed, where would those in need turn for assistance? How many people collect food and sell it? Where are they from? This sets up a criteria so you know what types of information to look for.

The second step is to seek out other people as both sources of information, and as feedback on your decision making process. Choose people who are not only knowledgeable but who will be able to provide you with objective commentary, including criticism. Discussion with others, whether one-on-one or in a group, can be an invaluable step in the process. You might discover better or more sources of data, find out about further options, or realize that you forgot an important aspect of the decision.

The third step is to play "what if?" Explore each option as a solution, asking yourself (and others, if appropriate) how would this option would work as a solution? Who would benefit? Who would be hurt, annoyed, or wronged? What is the best-case scenario and what is the worst for your option? Test each possibility and weigh its possible benefits and detriments. How do they measure up to the criteria you established in step one?

Example

Imagine you decided that the most important criteria for making your decision was whether or not those in need would get free food from some other source if the food pantry closed. In step three, you will ask questions such as, "are there other food pantries that are accessible to our town?" "Do those pantries limit their visitors to only those who live in their communities?" "Could we provide other assistance to those in our town to help them purchase food, such as gift certificates to grocery stores?"

TIP

Before making a judgment, establish your criteria. Be specific about what would make an idea a good one. What makes the action the right thing to do?

Practice

You inherited $5,000 from your great-aunt. You want to put the money into a mutual fund, but your spouse wants to use it to pay off a credit card debt. What information would be important to find out in preparing to make the judgment call as to what to do with the money? Circle as many as apply.

a. What is the year-to-date rate of return on the mutual fund?

b. How much interest does the credit card company charge you?

c. Which kinds of investments did your great-aunt favor?

d. Can you transfer your credit card balance to a card with a 0% interest rate?

Answer

Choices **a**, **b**, and **d** would be valuable information to have when preparing to make such judgment call. Choice **c** is not relevant.

What about Biases and Intuition?

Judgment calls are subjective, not simply a distillation of facts. Even after you get facts and explore the "what if" scenarios, the final decision is still your opinion. So to make good judgment calls, people need to acknowledge and check their natural biases. For example, someone might have lost a large part of his or her savings due to a drop in the stock market and become leery of investing. Or, perhaps the person grew up in a family that was never in debt and stressed the evils of credit. Such experiences could cloud a person's ability to make an effective judgment call about buying stock.

Any preexisting biases or attitudes reduce the ability to evaluate information objectively. Be aware of them. You can't eliminate them, but you can make sure they don't get in the way of a good judgment call.

What about intuition or instincts? As you go through the process of making a judgment call, you might get a feeling, a hunch, that one option simply feels right when compared to the others even when logic tells you otherwise. Also called a gut reaction, this feeling can lead to a great decision. It can also lead to a disaster. As with biases, acknowledge your intuition but take to it as one factor in many. It should not outweigh the facts and other input you gathered in steps 1 through 3.

Practice

Which two are NOT examples of using intuition to make a judgment call?

  a. Sam has to choose whether to go to the college near his hometown or a college 900 miles away where his best friend will be going. Sam's father recently had a heart attack, so Sam decides to go to the school closer to home.

  b. Mr. Wilcox had a ticket on a flight to Paris. At the last minute, he decided not to go. "Something told me not to go," he told reporters after the plane crashed, killing all on board.

  c. The night before a job interview, Pam dreams that she gets the job but someone there belittles her for not being smart enough. When she's offered the job, at a great salary, Pam turns it down. She tells a friend she doesn't want to work with people who think she's dumb.

  d. Fred wants to buy a new computer. He researches all the new models, and then shops around and chooses the best deal.

Answer

Choices **a** and **d** are not examples of intuition. Choosing to be close to an ill relative or buy the best computer at the best price are not hunches.

Making the Call

You can prepare as thoroughly as humanly possible before making a judgment call, getting input and information from dozens of sources, and evaluating each option as carefully as possible. But it still comes down to your opinion. How do you make the leap to a decision? Here are a couple more ideas that can help.

Evaluate the Risks

Look at each option in terms of risk. How much risk are you willing to take, and are you willing to suffer the consequences if you make the wrong choice? For example, you are considering buying shares of a stock. The choice is to buy, or not to buy. The best-case scenario is that you buy and the price skyrockets. The worst-case scenario is you buy and the price plummets. Notice that the risk occurs only if you make the purchase. Therefore, in this case, you need to decide if you can tolerate the risk of having the worst-case scenario occur. If you can't, you should not buy. Ask yourself if you take the risk, how much money can you afford to lose?

Here is another scenario: You are a manager who must hire two new employees. When you advertise the openings, you get dozens of resumes. Two of them belong to current employees who wish to move up to higher paying jobs with more responsibility. You know them and are impressed with their job performance. The top two resumes from the rest of the batch are graduates from prestigious business schools. However, they have no relevant work experience. Who do you hire?

Evaluate the decision in terms of risk. The current employees are known to you. If you hire them, there is little risk that they will not be able to perform well on the job. Based on your own observations, they are both conscientious individuals who are more than capable of doing well in the new positions. The other candidates are a riskier choice. Although they have the education, they lack experience. Will you have to spend countless hours training them? Will they be able to handle the job requirements successfully? You can only guess at the answers. If you want to make a judgment call based on what will be the least risk, you will hire the current employees.

TIP

To determine how high the stakes are, organizations consider costs, productivity, meeting contract obligations, and profit. People consider personal and financial reward, career growth, personal satisfaction, and personal values.

Examine the Consequences

Remember that judgment calls are subjective and debatable. Let's go back to the example of the food pantry. Once you have impartially looked at the situation and the facts surrounding it, the judgment call as to whether to limit those who can visit it, remain open as usual, or close the pantry down comes down to an opinion. Half of the committee believes they are providing a valuable service to the community and should continue to do so even though some people are taking advantage of them. Others believe they can't prevent visitors from selling the food they are giving away, so they should close. You could probably form a strong argument for either case, but what if you had to make a choice?

One way to help make such as decision is to focus on the consequences. Will anyone be helped or harmed by the decision? Weigh the value and term of the benefit or detriment—is it a convenience or inconvenience, or does it result in a long-term effect? If all options will result in some negative action or result, which is least negative? Putting your answers into a graphic organizer, such as a chart, can help you to weigh your options.

For example, Beth, an employee of a large accounting firm, notices that her company is falsifying the financial records of a client, a multinational corporation. Should she report the action and risk losing her job, or say nothing and allow criminal behavior to continue? This may seem like a black-and-white, right-or-wrong situation, but in essence it's a moral dilemma. Beth supports her family, including an ailing grandmother, and needs the job. Let's explore her options on a chart.

By exploring her options, she understands that whistle-blowing could result in possible short-term negative effects for herself (unemployment). Of course, the other consequence is that the wrongdoing would stop and the criminals who falsified the records would probably be punished. In effect, she might save shareholders of the client's company millions of dollars.

But if she says nothing, her job will be secure, and there is a risk that someone outside the company will discover the illegal activity. If that happens, there could be major consequences not just for the person who falsified the records but for the entire company. Beth needs to carefully weigh the options in terms of possible consequences before she makes the judgment call.

Option 1: Report Wrongdoing

Who is helped?	company	Long/short term?	Short (get rid of bad employee)
Who is harmed?	self	Long/short term?	Short (might lose job)

Option 2: Keep Quiet

Who is helped?	self	Long/short term?	Long (career stable)
Who is harmed?	company	Long/short term?	Long (wrongdoing continues)

Practice

Use a chart to explore the possible consequences of each option in the following scenario.

The owner of a small store finds out that his best employee, a college student, closed the store an hour early over the weekend so she could attend a party. This employee has consistently been an excellent, dependable worker, and is the only one the owner can trust to close the store in his absence. In fact, finding reliable help is very difficult. However, by closing an hour early, the employee cost the store-owner a few hundred dollars in profits, based on typical Saturday night sales. Should the store-owner confront the employee about the early closing? Fire her? Pretend it didn't happen?

Option 1:

Who is helped?	Long/short term?
Who is harmed?	Long/short term?

Option 2:

Who is helped?	Long/short term?
Who is harmed?	Long/short term?

Option 3:

Who is helped?	Long/short term?
Who is harmed?	Long/short term?

Answer

Remember that with judgment calls, there is not always one right answer. However, a good response is one that adequately explores all three options and their possible consequences.

Option 1: Confront the Employee

Who is helped?	store owner	Long/short term?	Long (won't lose profits again)
Who is harmed?	store owner	Long/short term?	Long (might lose employee)

Option 2: Fire Employee

Who is helped?	no one	Long/short term?	
Who is harmed?	store owner	Long/short term?	Possibly long (won't easily replace employee, will have to do more work himself)

Option 3: Say Nothing

Who is helped?	employee	Long/short term?	Long (won't be embarrassed about incident, will keep job)
Who is harmed?	store owner	Long/short term?	Both (might lose more profits from early closings)

In Short

Judgment calls can be difficult. In a situation where the stakes are high, and even the experts disagree, you may not want to make a choice that is, at best, subjective and debatable. But there are many circumstances in which you will have to do just that. You will need to consider any facts you can gather, the advice of others, your intuition, and even your values. Take your time with judgment calls, and with practice, you will become more confident in making them.

Skill Building Until Next Time

- Judges frequently make judgment calls, even though they rely on evidence and prior decisions. Check a newspaper for a recent, complicated case, and then find out more about it online. Look at the evidence presented by both sides. On what do you think the judge based his or her decision? Would you have made the same decision?
- Do you know anyone who has downloaded music from the Internet without permission? Was the decision a judgment call? If so, how did the person come to the decision?

18 ▶ EXPLANATION OR ARGUMENT?

Discussion is an exchange of knowledge; argument an exchange of ignorance.

Robert Quillen, American journalist and humorist (1887–1948)

LESSON SUMMARY

So far, we've talked a lot about arguments—things like how to make them, what makes them valid or invalid, and how people use misleading techniques in them. In this lesson, you'll discover how to tell the difference between an argument and an explanation. You'll also find out how to judge explanations—what makes them effective or ineffective.

Ever hear or say this before? "You've got some explaining to do!" We all, at one time or another, have had to explain ourselves or hear explanations from others. It might have been a simple incident, like showing up late to a movie. Other times, an explanation can make or break things, or end up with a terrible result. We often take explanations for granted, thinking we can explain our way out of anything. But, as with arguments, explanations can be effective or ineffective. They can get someone off the hook, or deeper into trouble. It's important to understand what a good explanation is, and how it differs from an argument.

What Is an Explanation?

At first glance, this seems like a simple question. Someone asks, "Why did you do that?" Your reply is an explanation, giving reasons why you did what you did. But basically, an explanation is a statement or set of statements that give new information about something that's been accepted as fact. When answering the question, "Why did you do that?" you won't say you didn't do it, which would be an argument. It's an accepted fact that you did something, so you have to give information about why you did it.

An explanation has two parts: what will be explained, called the *explanadum*; and the statements that do the explaining, called the *explanans*. To answer the question, "Why did you buy that car?" someone might explain, "I bought it because it gets great gas mileage." The phrase "I bought it" is the explanadum. "It gets great gas mileage" is the explanan.

When an explanation is accepted, it removes or lessens a problem. The "why?" is solved. In the previous example, the person asking the question does not understand something (why someone bought a certain car). After the explanation, he or she will. In addition, a good explanation is relevant. That is, it speaks directly to the issue. If someone asks, "Why are you late?" and you reply, "I was late because my shirt is blue," you have given a poor explanation. It is not relevant to the question asked.

The four qualities of a good explanation are:

1. it gives new information
2. the topic is accepted as fact
3. when given, it removes or lessens a problem
4. it is relevant

In Lesson 13, you learned about the fallacy of circular reasoning. "I like chocolate chip because it is my favorite flavor" is an example of circular reasoning, because the premise (it is my favorite flavor) is the same as saying the conclusion (I like chocolate chip).

Explanations may be circular as well. When they are, they offer no new information.

Example
I did well on my SATs because I got a high score.

The explanadum and the explanans simply repeat each other. Doing well on a test and getting a high score are different ways of saying the same thing. In order to make this an effective explanation, the speaker would have to give new information. We already know she did well on the test, but why? She might say:

I did well on my SATs because I studied and got enough rest before the test.

This explanation works because the explanans tell something new. It also fulfills the other three qualities of a good explanation: It is about something that is not disputed (the speaker did well on the SATs), it solves the problem of not knowing why the person did well, and it's relevant (the reasons make sense). If the speaker had said, "I did well on my SATs because I have a dog that won't walk on a leash," we would say the explanation was irrelevant. Having a dog has nothing to do with doing well on a standardized test.

Practice
How could you revise the following weak explanations to make them strong?

1. Everyone on our street is without electricity because our power went out.

_____

_____

2. My new MP3 player is not working since I ate that ice cream sundae.

_____

_____

Answer

1. A good explanation would give reasons, or new information, about the power outage. Responses might be "because Hurricane Graham hit here yesterday," or "because the wiring is old and needs to be replaced."

2. To make a good explanation, you would have to give relevant reasons as to why the MP3 player is not working, such as, "since my brother dropped it" or "since the battery went dead."

Distinguishing an Explanation from an Argument

You know that a good explanation gives new, relevant information about an accepted fact that is problematic or puzzling. So it's usually easy to spot an explanation that doesn't work on one or more of these points. But it can be tricky when an argument masquerades as an explanation, or an explanation looks like an argument.

An explanation answers the question, "why?" and helps you understand something by telling what caused it. An argument, on the other hand, tries to convince you of the truth of a conclusion by giving reasons (premises) that are evidence for the conclusion. Simply put, an explanation provides causes, and an argument provides evidence. Even when you understand this basic difference, it can sometimes be difficult to tell one from the other. Why is it important to know the difference? Someone might label his or her explanation as an argument, trying to convince you of something by telling you its causes, as opposed to giving you evidence. So knowing three specific ways in which explanations and arguments differ is important.

Recommendations and Value Judgments

Many arguments express a recommendation, or value judgment, and try to convince you of the goodness or rightness of it. Explanations do not contain such recommendations or judgments. They are about undisputed facts and not attempts at persuasion. For example, here is a conclusion to an argument:

> The best place for a steak is Louie's Steak Shack. They use only high quality meat, and the décor is fabulous.

How do we know this isn't an explanation? It is the speaker's judgment and recommendation, an opinion rather than a fact. The statement could become an explanation if there were facts that the restaurant was "the best place for a steak." For example, state another person's opinion: "*Eat-Out* magazine says the best place for a steak is Louie's Steak Shack because it has only high quality meat, and the décor is fabulous."

Now we have a simple statement of fact, what the magazine says, followed by its causes, why the magazine has that opinion—the quality of the meat and the décor. Always remember that explanations are about an already-accepted fact. Judgments and recommendations aren't facts.

Practice

Tell if the underlined text is a fact or a judgment.

____ 1. <u>My science grades have been really low.</u> I think I'm going to flunk.

____ 2. With such a great menu and prices, <u>this restaurant will be a great success.</u>

____ 3. <u>The local no-smoking ban should be lifted</u> because adults can decide for themselves whether or not to smoke.

____ 4. I was late for work yesterday because <u>I overslept and missed my bus.</u>

Answers

1. fact
2. judgment
3. judgment
4. fact

Feelings and Beliefs

Distinguishing between arguments and explanations can be tricky if they involve statements about how someone thinks, feels, or what he or she believes. Since explanations aren't value judgments or recommendations, you wouldn't expect to see words like "believe" or "feel" in them, but you might. For example, you're thinking about buying stock in a company where two of your friends work. One tells you, "The company is doing really well. Sales are high, and one of our products won an award." The other says, "Economists believe our company is doing really well because our sales are high, and one of our products won an award." The word "believe" is a warning signal that the statement is an opinion. But look closely. Whose belief is it? Your friend isn't one of the economists. She is simply stating a fact—that economists hold that belief.

The first friend is trying to convince you that her conclusion is valid by giving you evidence. The second is explaining the reasons why a group of people believe something. Perhaps you won't buy the stock after either friends' statement, but if you are thinking critically, you know the motivation of each.

Fast Forward

What about the future? If someone is talking about what will happen tomorrow, you might think it must be an argument. Explanations are about undisputed facts, and arguments are about judgments and opinions. Can there be a fact about something that has not even happened yet? The answer is yes. Just because you see the words "tomorrow," "next week," or "someday" does not mean you are looking at an argument.

Here are a few examples of explanadums about the future:

When Evidence Is Missing

When do people tend to use an explanation when they really need to make an argument? When they are trying to justify an opinion. Think about the persuasive advertisements examined in Lesson 9. When an advertiser wants to convince you to buy his or her product, he or she needs an argument with evidence. But typically, there is no evidence. One detergent is just as good as another; one brand of tires performs equally with other brands. How, then, can the advertiser construct an argument without evidence? By using explanations that either give no new information, or give irrelevant information, such as "our dish detergent is much better than Brand X, because it smells like lemons." When you see through these types of claims, you are distinguishing between explanations and evidence. Critical-thinking skills help you to understand that weak or unsubstantiated explanations are no substitute for scarce or missing evidence.

This fall, the leaves will turn colors before dropping to the ground.

Someday, we will all die.

I am going to turn 25 next week.

The point is that facts are not just about things that have already happened. There are many things about the future that we can accept with certainty. When you pay careful attention to the context of the argument or explanation, you can tell the difference between the two, regardless of whether they have to do with last week or next week.

Practice

Label each statement as an (**A**) argument or an (**E**) explanation.

___ **1.** We should not have school on Saturdays because we need time for recreation.

___ **2.** The reason my credit rating is high is because I never make late payments.

___ **3.** If you worked out more, you would lose weight, because exercise burns calories.

___ **4.** The death penalty should be abolished because two wrongs do not make a right.

Answers

1. Argument

2. Explanation

3. Explanation

4. Argument

TIP

Remember to say exactly what you mean. If your words are confusing to listeners, they won't know if you're giving an explanation or an argument.

In Short

Good explanations are helpful. They give people the information they need to solve problems and understand situations. They differ from arguments in a number of key ways. Explanations answer the question, "why?" by giving reasons that are the causes of a particular fact. Arguments try to convince you of their conclusions by presenting evidence for them. While explanations are about facts, arguments can be value judgments or recommendations. Understanding these differences allows you to see through poor arguments that aim to convince you to do, buy, or think something based on little or no evidence. Being able to recognize and formulate good explanations is a valuable critical-thinking skill.

Skill Building Until Next Time

- Listen for explanations in conversations with friends and family. How often do you hear irrelevant explanans or circular reasoning?
- Imagine you want to start a small business. You have no experience, and you need funding from your bank. How would you explain your idea to a bank loan officer?

19 ▶ CRITICAL THINKING FOR EXAMS

Examinations are formidable even to the best prepared, for the greatest fool may ask more than the wisest man can answer.

Charles Caleb Colton, English writer and minister (1780–1832)

LESSON SUMMARY

Did you know that people applying for jobs or job promotions take critical-thinking exams somewhat like the ones college-bound students take? More and more businesses, including state and local governments, test the critical skills of prospective employees to measure their ability to handle problems on the job. In this lesson, you'll discover what some of those critical-thinking test questions are like. And you'll learn how you can use this book to help you prepare to ace these tests.

Most college-bound high school students are familiar with the ACT and the SAT, tests that many colleges and universities use to make admissions decisions. And college graduates may take tests like the GRE, GMAT, and LSAT to get into graduate school. All these tests have a section that measures critical-thinking skills through a variety of questions based on reading passages, scientific experiments, and written opinions and arguments. Many of the tests are similar: ACT critical reading questions are similar to those on the SAT, and the GRE Analytical Writing Test is comparable to parts of the GMAT and LSAT. So in this lesson, we will focus on sections of each test that are unique.

The SAT Reasoning Test

The SAT is divided into three parts: critical reading, math, and writing. The critical reading section includes short and long reading passages, followed by questions that test your ability to comprehend the content. Questions may be based on one or two reading passages, and some are not based on any passage, but instead measure your knowledge of word meaning and logical sentence structure.

What You Will Find on the Test

The SAT passages represent various writing styles and are taken from different disciplines, including the humanities, social sciences, and natural sciences. They are written at the college level, which means they are sophisticated and complex, and may contain some unfamiliar vocabulary. It is not expected that you have any prior knowledge of the material in the passages, but rather that you have the ability to read, understand, and use the information in them. Each SAT also contains a pair of related passages presented as one reading section. They may express opposite points of view, support each other's point of view, or otherwise complement each other.

Critical reading questions will direct you to:

- infer the meaning of words from context
- comprehend the information presented in the passage
- analyze the information
- critique the authors' arguments (singly and as opposed to one another in a dual passage section)

Using This Book to Prepare for the SAT

Lessons that relate directly to skills needed for success on the SAT Critical Reading section are:

- **Lessons 1 and 3: Inference.** These lessons cover how to take in information, and understand what it suggests, but does not say outright. When you infer, you draw conclusions based on evidence.
- **Lesson 9: Persuasion Techniques.** Some questions will ask you to evaluate arguments. Understanding how persuasion works, and being able to identify rhetorical devices used in persuasive writing, will help you to correctly answer these types of questions.
- **Lessons 12 and 14: Deductive and Inductive Reasoning.** These lessons teach the design of logical arguments. They will both help you recognize such arguments, and show you how to make them yourself.
- **Lessons 13, 15, and 16: Logical Fallacies.** Knowing the terminology of fallacies, and how they work, will help you identify and describe weak or invalid arguments with accuracy.
- **Lesson 17: Judgment Calls.** This lesson also teaches about inference. When you have some evidence, but not enough to come to a clear-cut decision, you will need to make a judgment about the answer.

Roadblocks to Critical Reading Question Success

1. **Using prior information.** Every answer comes from a reading selection, whether it appears directly or can be inferred. If you have prior knowledge of the subject, don't use it. Adding information, even if it makes sense to you to do so, can lead you to the wrong answer.

2. **Choosing an answer just because it is true.** There may be a couple of true answers, but only one will answer the question best.

Practice

The following excerpt tells of a defining chapter in the life of a budding scientist.

The voyage of the "Beagle" has been by far the most important event in my life, and has determined my whole career; yet it depended on so small a circumstance as my uncle offering to drive (5) me 30 miles to Shrewsbury, which few uncles would have done, and on such a trifle as the shape of my nose. I have always felt that I owe to the voyage the first real training or education of my mind; I was led to attend closely to several (10) branches of natural history, and thus my powers of observation were improved, though they were always fairly developed.

The investigation of the geology of all the places visited was far more important, as reason- (15) ing here comes into play. On first examining a new district nothing can appear more hopeless than the chaos of rocks; but by recording the stratification and nature of the rocks and fossils at many points, always reasoning and predicting (20) what will be found elsewhere, light soon begins to dawn on the district, and the structure of the whole becomes more or less intelligible. I had brought with me the first volume of Lyell's 'Principles of Geology,' which I studied attentively; and (25) the book was of the highest service to me in many ways. The very first place that I examined, namely St. Jago in the Cape de Verde islands, showed me clearly the wonderful superiority of Lyell's manner of treating geology, compared with that of any other author, whose works I had with (30) me or ever afterwards read. Another of my occupations was collecting animals of all classes, briefly describing and roughly dissecting many of the marine ones; but from not being able to draw, and from not having sufficient anatomical knowl- (35) edge, a great pile of manuscripts which I made during the voyage has proved almost useless. I thus lost much time, with the exception of that spent in acquiring some knowledge of the Crustaceans, as this was of service when in after years (40) I undertook a monograph of the Cirripedia.

During some part of the day I wrote my Journal, and took much pains in describing carefully and vividly all that I had seen; and this was good practice. My Journal served also, in part, (45) as letters to my home, and portions were sent to England whenever there was an opportunity.

The above various special studies were, however, of no importance compared with the habit of energetic industry and of concentrated attention (50) to whatever I was engaged in, which I then acquired. Everything about which I thought or read was made to bear directly on what I had seen or was likely to see; and this habit of mind was continued during the five years of the voyage. I (55) feel sure that it was this training which has enabled me to do whatever I have done in science.

Looking backwards, I can now perceive how my love for science gradually preponderated over every other taste. (60)

1. In lines 8–9, when the author speaks of "the first real training or education of my mind," he refers to
   a. the voyage of the Beagle.
   b. the development of his career.
   c. the branches of natural history.
   d. his powers of observation.
   e. the shape of his nose.

2. In lines 13–14, the author says he considers geology far more important due to the fact that
   a. its structure is obvious.
   b. it helped him learn to reason.
   c. he made sense out of chaos.
   d. play is as important as work.
   e. he learned how to study.

3. In line 18, the word *stratification* most nearly means
   a. coloration.
   b. calcification.
   c. layers.
   d. composition.
   e. location.

4. In lines 21–22, the phrase *the structure of the whole becomes more or less intelligible* refers to
   a. the break of day.
   b. the ability to predict findings.
   c. a comprehensive knowledge.
   d. the assurance of correctness.
   e. the fitting together of disparate facts.

5. In line 37, the admission that many of the author's manuscripts proved almost useless depends on the notion that
   a. it is necessary to draw and know anatomy when collecting animals.
   b. additional description would have been required for clarity.
   c. a rough dissection is better than no dissection.
   d. publication requires more finesse than he possessed.
   e. describing and dissection are a waste of time.

6. In line 41, the word *monograph* most nearly means
   a. a line drawing.
   b. a comprehensive treatment.
   c. a one-page summary.
   d. a thorough dissection.
   e. a written treatment.

7. In lines 42–45, the author sees the primary value of his journal as being
   a. a contribution to English society.
   b. good preparation for his future work.
   c. practice in painstaking description.
   d. killing two birds with one stone.
   e. to serve as letters home.

8. In line 59–60, the word *preponderated* most nearly means
   a. predominated.
   b. postponed.
   c. graduated.
   d. eliminated.
   e. assuaged.

Answers

1. d. It was the training in several branches of natural history that led to the improvement of the author's powers of observation (lines 10–11).

2. b. The author says the investigation of geology brought reasoning into play (lines 14–15), meaning he had to develop his reasoning.

3. c. *Stratification* means layers. In lines 17–19 stratification is opposed to *chaos,* as the way in which rocks are ordered.

4. e. As the author works through the logic of geology, the many disparate facts begin to make sense (lines 21–22).

5. a. The author says that the facts that he was not able to draw and did not have sufficient anatomical knowledge (lines 34–37) made his manuscripts worthless.

6. e. *Monograph* is a word for a narrowly focused written treatment of a subject. Compare *monograph* (line 41) with *manuscript* (line 36) for your context clue. In the context, a monograph could not be less thorough than a manuscript.

7. c. The author says he took much pains in describing carefully and vividly, and that this was good practice (lines 42–45).

8. a. The word *preponderated* means took over or predominated. In line 60 the word *over* placed after preponderated is your clue, along with the context of the sentence.

ACT

The ACT consists of four separate tests: English, reading, math, and science. The reading test is similar to the SAT Critical Reading Test; it consists of passages followed by questions that relate to them. The science test also involves critical-thinking skills. It is designed as a reasoning test, rather than an assessment of your science knowledge. As with the critical reading tests, you are given in the passages all the information you need to know to answer the questions. (However, the ACT website does note that "background knowledge acquired in general, introductory science courses is needed to answer some of the questions.")

What You Will Find on the Test

The ACT Science Reasoning Test contains 40 questions covering biology, chemistry, physics, and Earth/space sciences, including geology, astronomy, and meteorology. The questions measure interpretation, analysis, evaluation, reasoning, and problem-solving skills. There are seven passages that present scientific information in one of three formats: data representation (graphs, tables, etc.), research summaries, or conflicting viewpoints (several related but inconsistent hypotheses or views). Each passage is followed by a number of multiple-choice questions that ask you to interpret, evaluate, analyze, draw conclusions, and make predictions about the information. Here, "passages" may include both text and graphics, like figures, charts, diagrams, tables, or any combination of these.

Specifically, you will be asked to:

- read and understand scatter plots, graphs, tables, diagrams, charts, figures, etc.
- interpret scatter plots, graphs, tables, diagrams, charts, figures, etc.
- compare and interpret information presented in graphics
- draw conclusions about the information provided
- make predictions about the data
- develop hypotheses based on the data

Using This Book to Prepare for the Exam

- **Lessons 1 and 2: Recognizing and Defining Problems.** These lessons will help you to zero in on the precise problems presented in Conflicting Viewpoint passages.

- **Lesson 3: Focused Observation.** Knowing how to concentrate and approach a problem thoroughly is critical, because not only are you expected to arrive at the correct answer, but you must record it in a relatively short period.

- **Lesson 4: Graphic Organizers.** Understanding how information fits into charts, maps, and outlines will help you to make sense of, and draw conclusions about, them.

- **Lesson 9: Persuasion Techniques.** This lesson will be most useful when dealing with Conflicting Viewpoints. It explains how persuasive arguments work. Having this knowledge will help you to be better able to analyze conflicting viewpoints.

- **Lesson 10: The Numbers Game.** As with lesson 4, you will gain an understanding of how numbers are used and misused. Many questions are designed to evaluate how good your skills in this area are.

- **Lessons 12 and 14: Deductive and Inductive Reasoning.** These lessons cover the structure of logical arguments, which help you draw conclusions, and, with inductive logic, the development of hypotheses.

- **Lesson 17: Judgment Calls.** Any time you make an inference, you are testing your ability to make sound judgment calls. This lesson will also help you to evaluate the consequences of possible solutions.

- **Lesson 18: Explanations.** In this lesson, you discovered what makes a valid, sound explanation. On tests, you're often asked to choose the best answer out of four. With what you've learned, you'll be able to pick the right answer.

Practice

*Read the following debate, which took place **before** scientists officially decided Pluto was not a planet, then answer the questions.*

Scientist 1

Based on perturbations in Neptune's orbit, the search for a ninth planet was conducted and Pluto was discovered in 1930. Pluto orbits the Sun just as the other eight planets do, it has a moon, Charon, and a stable orbit. Based on its distance from the Sun, Pluto should be grouped with the planets known as gas giants. In addition, Pluto, like the planet Mercury, has little or no atmosphere. Pluto is definitely not a comet because it does not have a tail like a comet when it is near the Sun. Pluto is also not an asteroid, although its density is closer to an asteroid than to any of the other planets. Pluto is a planet because it has been classified as one for more than sixty years since its discovery.

Scientist 2

Pluto should no longer be classified as a planet based on new evidence that has come to light in the last few years. When Pluto was first discovered, nothing was known about its orbit or its composition. Pluto has an orbit that is not in the same plane as the other planets (i.e., it is tilted) and its orbit is more eccentric, or elongated than any other planet's orbit. Pluto orbits the Sun in the outer solar system, and so should be similar in size and composition to the gas giants, but it is not. Pluto lacks the rings that all other gas giants possess. Also, Pluto's moon is larger than any other moon relative to its parent planet. In recent years, new objects have been found which belong to the Kuiper Belt, a region of small solid icy bodies that orbit the Sun beyond the orbit of Neptune and Pluto. A large object called Quaoar has recently been discovered which has a density nearly identical to Pluto, Charon, and Triton. Based on these facts, I conclude that Pluto is a Kuiper Belt object.

TIP

Always read all directions carefully and read all the answers before choosing one. Answer the easy questions first. And don't change an answer unless you're sure it's wrong; your first guess is most often right.

1. Scientist 1 states that "Based on its distance from the Sun, Pluto should be grouped with the planets knows as gas giants." Which of the following statements made by Scientist 2 opposes Scientist 1's belief that Pluto is a gas planet?
   a. Pluto's moon is larger than any other moon relative to its parent planet.
   b. A large object called Quaoar has recently been discovered which has a density nearly identical to Pluto, Charon, and Triton.
   c. Pluto has an orbit that is not in the same plane as the other planets (i.e., it is tilted) and its orbit is more eccentric, or elongated than any other planet's orbit.
   d. Pluto lacks rings that all other gas giants possess.

2. What do both scientists agree upon?
   a. Pluto is like Mercury.
   b. Pluto is a Kuiper Belt Object.
   c. Pluto orbits the sun.
   d. Charon is a planet.

3. Which of the following are reasons why Scientist 2 believes Pluto should NOT be classified as a planet?
   I. Pluto has no atmosphere.
   II. Pluto is similar in composition to Quaoar.
   III. Pluto has the most eccentric orbit of all the planets.
   IV. Pluto's orbit is not in the same plane as the orbits of the other planets.
   a. II, III only
   b. I, III, IV
   c. III, IV only
   d. II, III, IV

4. Based on composition and density, Pluto is a
   a. Kuiper Belt Object.
   b. Earth-like planet.
   c. comet.
   d. gas giant planet.

5. Based on the information presented by Scientist 2, what is a possible origin for Neptune's moon, Triton?
   a. Triton is a natural moon of Neptune.
   b. Triton is a captured Kuiper Belt Object.
   c. Triton is a captured asteroid.
   d. Triton is a captured comet.

Answers

1. **d.** Only the statement "Pluto lacks the rings that all other gas giants possess," opposes the statement made by Scientist 1.

2. **c.** If you read both passages carefully, only one fact appears in both. Scientist 1 states, "Pluto orbits the Sun just as the other eight planets do," and Scientist 2 states, "Pluto orbits the Sun in the outer solar system."

3. d. According to Scientist 2, the factors that separate Pluto are its different density, composition, and orbital characteristics, which are more like those of the Kuiper Belt Objects than the planets.

4. a. Pluto, Charon, and Neptune's moon, Triton, all have densities and compositions similar to the newly discovered object Quaoar. This infers that they are all bodies originally from the Kuiper Belt.

5. b. Triton's similar density and composition to Quaoar are evidence that indicate that it is an object that was captured by Neptune's gravity at some point in the early formation of the solar system.

GRE (Graduate Record Examinations) General Test

The GRE General Test assesses knowledge and skills needed for graduate study. There are four parts: verbal reasoning, quantitative reasoning, critical thinking, and analytical writing skills not related to any specific field of study. The verbal section is similar to the critical reading on the SAT. You're asked to analyze, evaluate, and synthesize information in passages you read.

What You Will Find on the Test

The GRE analytical writing section differs from both the SAT and ACT in that there are no multiple-choice questions. Instead, your critical-thinking skills are tested as you examine claims and evidence, support ideas with relevant reasons and examples, and keep up a rational, well-focused discussion. Answers are judged on how well you:

- consider the complexities and implications of the issue
- organize, develop, and express your ideas on the issue
- identify and analyze important features of the argument
- organize, develop, and express your critique of the argument
- support your ideas with relevant reasons and examples
- control the elements of standard written English

The Issue section provides two opinions on topics of general interest. You must select one and then respond to it from any perspective. Your response must be supported with sound explanations, evidence, and examples. In the next section, you are given an argument to analyze. Rather than giving your opinion on the subject, you must explain how the argument is either logically sound or not.

Using This Book to Prepare for the Test

- **Lessons 1 and 2: Recognizing and Defining Problems.** These lessons will help you to zero in on the precise problems you will discuss in both the opinion and argument sections. It is especially important that you can make the distinction between a problem and its symptoms or consequences.
- **Lesson 3: Focused Observation.** Knowing how to gather information is critical, because you must back up your opinion or critique with relevant examples and reasoning.
- **Lesson 8: Fact and Opinion.** You won't have access to research materials while taking the GRE, but you can think critically about the documentation of sources and credentials. If the author of the argument you must analyze cites facts and figures without documentation, that is an important point for you to make.

- **Lesson 9: Persuasion Techniques.** This lesson teaches you how to recognize and describe persuasion techniques. You will learn the names of the rhetorical devices used in persuasive writing, and how they work. The use of these correct terms will improve the quality of your responses.

- **Lesson 10: The Numbers Game.** Surveys, studies, and statistics may be used in the argument you must analyze. Knowing how to judge the validity of such facts will help you to construct a strong response (see the following sample argument and response for a specific example).

- **Lessons 12 and 14: Deductive and Inductive Reasoning.** These lessons cover the structure of logical arguments. You need a thorough understanding of reasoning to be able to identify and analyze the important features of the argument you are given.

- **Lesson 18: Explanations.** There are no "correct" answers on the GRE Analytical Writing Test. Whatever view or critique you decide to write about, you will need to explain yourself using evidence and examples. This lesson teaches you how to recognize and construct sound explanations.

Top-Score Sample Argument Essay and Response

Prompt

The following appeared in a letter to the editor in the sports pages of a community newspaper.

A teacher can't earn more than $50,000 a year doing one of the toughest jobs in the world. These saints work a lot harder and deserve to get paid a lot more for the miracles they perform on a daily basis. The average salary for professional athletes is $650,000. That's more than ten times what the average public high school principal makes. Basketball players can earn millions in just one season, and football players can earn hundreds of thousands for just a 30-second commercial. Even benchwarmers make more in a month than teachers. Who is more important—the woman who taught you how to read and write so that you can succeed in life, or the jock who plays for a living?

Response

The author of this piece drives home the idea that professional athletes get paid too much, especially in comparison to teachers, who help you "succeed in life." As much as anyone may believe that teachers deserve to be paid more than they earn, or that some professional athletes are grossly overpaid, the argument this author makes is not very effective. Much of the evidence and reasoning used by the author of this piece is flimsy and illogically reasoned—there is a shaky conclusion, counterarguments are not addressed, and the premises the author uses to support the conclusion are not reasonably qualified.

The conclusion drawn in this argument is, "These saints work a lot harder and deserve to get paid a lot more for the miracles they perform on a daily basis." This sentence raises several red flags. First of all, the author draws a comparison between teachers and saints. It is true that teachers do noble work, and arguably this work improves individuals and sometimes even society; however, neither of these duties makes teachers "saints." Second of all, the author uses the word *miracles* to describe the results of teachers' work. This word is emotionally charged, implying that a teacher's work is amazing and fantastic. The connotation of the word *miracle* suggests bias in the author's opinion of the teaching profession. Juxtaposed to calling the work of professional athletes "play," this word draws on the reader's compassion, appealing to emotional rather than presenting impartial evidence. Finally, this claim is incomplete. Teachers work harder than whom? Deserve to get paid more than whom? Although the answer "professional athletes" is implied, the claim does not explicitly state this.

The argument as given is weakened by the fact that it does not address any counterarguments or note any other perspectives. It could have addressed the positive role models many athletes play to youth, the community outreach many professional athletes do for free, or the generous charities many athletes set up and donate money to. By stating some of these counterarguments and refuting them, the author could have gained more credibility, showing that insight and logic played into his or her argument. As it is, the argument appears biased and one-sided.

What's more, the premises the author based his or her conclusions on seem unreasonably qualified. For example, the average salary given for professional athletes doesn't seem like the appropriate measure to use in this situation. There are many professional sports, professional table tennis or volleyball, for example, where the salaries for even the top players don't approach $650,000. If you were to survey all professional athletes, you'd probably find that the typical player doesn't come close to a six-figure salary. However, because high-profile athletes like Shaquille O'Neal and Tiger Woods make millions of dollars, the average is higher than the typical salary. Therefore, this piece of evidence the author chooses seems loaded.

In addition, sources are not provided for this salary statistic. The author does not cite sources for the $50,000 teacher's salary or that benchwarmers make more than teachers. (Besides, it is unlikely that table tennis team benchwarmers make larger salaries than teachers!) Because this evidence lacks sources, the author's credibility is weakened, since the evidence cannot be verified as fact. If the figures can be verified, then the premises are reasonable; however, for all the reader knows, the author simply made everything up.

Overall, this argument is not well reasoned. The conclusion of this argument seems biased and the word choice seems suspect, appealing to emotion rather than logic. Additionally, the argument does not seem to consider alternate viewpoints, further weakening its position. Finally, the evidence presented in the argument weakens its credibility because it doesn't cite a source to verify its validity. Although many people believe that teachers deserve to be paid a better salary, this particular argument isn't effective. The logical conclusion would be to suggest some type of change or solution to this problem, but the incomplete conclusion, appealing to emotion makes it sound like the author is complaining, rather than making a good case for a teacher salary increase.

Vocational and Other Critical Thinking Tests

In addition to the tests already discussed in this lesson, many colleges, universities, and businesses use critical-thinking tests, such as the California Critical Thinking Test or the Cornell Critical Thinking Test. Employers use these kinds of tests to help make hiring and promotion decisions. Here are several examples of the kinds of questions you might find.

Practice

1. Some workers in the factory are women. Most of the women in the factory have children. Marsha works in the factory. Conclusion: Marsha has children.
   a. necessarily true
   b. probably, but not necessarily true
   c. can't be determined
   d. probably, but not necessarily false
   e. necessarily false

2. Suppose you know that:

all the books about cooking are Cindy's.

all the blue books are Cindy's.

Then would this be true?

At least some of the blue books are about cooking.

  a. yes

  b. no

  c. maybe

Answers

1. The correct answer is choice **c**. You can't decide without more information, because you don't know how what "some" and "many" are.
2. The correct answer is choice **c**. Cindy might have a collection of books about cooking and a separate set of books that are blue.

To prepare for this type of test, review in particular the lessons on deductive and inductive reasoning, as well as the lessons on logical fallacies.

A widely used test, in both vocational and educational settings, is the Watson-Glaser Critical Thinking Appraisal (WGCTA). It is made up of various reading passages followed by questions designed to test these skills:

- inference
- recognition of assumptions
- deduction
- interpretation
- evaluation of arguments

This test is similar to many other critical reading evaluations. You can prepare for the WCGTA by using this book as explained in the SAT and ACT sections already discussed.

Many vocational tests, such as the Corrections Officer Exam and the U.S. Customs Service Critical Thinking Skills Test, use situational questions. You read a written scenario, and then you must answer questions. The questions may ask you to make inferences or judgment calls. There are three types of situational questions:

1. read rules or agency procedures and apply them to a hypothetical situation
2. answer which hypothetical situation is most likely to indicate dangerous or criminal activity
3. read about a job-related situation and choose which of five inferences is correct, and why it is correct

These tests rely heavily on the skills covered in Lessons 1, 2, and 3. You need to understand the problem or situation clearly and be able to determine what is implied, or may be inferred about it. Focused observation is a highly important skill in these types of jobs. Being able to make sound judgment calls (Lesson 17) is also critical. Here is an example taken from a situational reasoning part of a Corrections Officer Test.

Practice

Following are a set of rules and procedures for corrections officers. Based on these, answer the questions that follow them. You may refer back to the rules and procedures as often as needed.

- Contraband is any item that an inmate is not permitted to have in his or her possession. Officers who discover contraband will confiscate the item(s), investigate the situation, and write a report. Appropriate disciplinary action should be taken based on the results of the investigation. Pat-down searches of visitors to prison facilities should be performed whenever an officer receives a tip that a visitor may be attempting to smuggle contraband into the facility.

- Corrections officers are often responsible for seeing to it that inmates follow personal grooming rules. An officer can direct an inmate to get a haircut. To do so:

1. The officer should approach the inmate and tell the inmate a haircut is needed.
2. The officer should write a pass for the inmate to report to the desk supervisor.
3. The inmate reports to the desk supervisor, who records the inmate's presence in a log and then directs the inmate to wait in line for the haircut.
4. After the haircut, the inmate will report back to the officer who ordered the procedure.

Inmates housed in isolation are to be given the opportunity to shower every other day. The officer in charge of this procedure should document the time, date, and name of the inmate who showered.

1. Jewelry is considered contraband in prison environments. Officer Nolan conducts a search of Inmate Harland's cell and finds a gold ring under his pillow. What should he do?

   a. He should confiscate the ring and tell Inmate Harland that he can have it back when he is released from prison.

   b. He should leave it where it is because Inmate Harland might accuse him of planting the ring in his cell.

   c. He should confiscate the ring and tell Inmate Harland that he won't report it as a violation, but now Inmate Harland "owes him one."

   d. He should confiscate the ring, find out how Inmate Harland got it, and then write a report detailing the incident.

2. Inmate Greggs's hair is hanging below the bottom of his collar. Officer Trunkle orders Inmate Greggs to get a haircut. What is the next step for Officer Trunkle to take?

   a. Check Inmate Greggs's cell mate to see if he needs a haircut.

   b. Call his supervisor to see if he can send Inmate Greggs to the barber.

   c. Check to see if the barber has an appointment open for Inmate Greggs.

   d. Write a pass to the desk supervisor for Inmate Greggs.

Answers

1. d.
2. d.

In Short

The skills you have learned in this book are invaluable when taking many kinds of exams. Those needed to gain admission to colleges and graduate schools are examples. Many such tests include sections on critical reading and writing in which you will be asked to make inferences, interpret graphic organizers, choose appropriate conclusions, and analyze arguments.

There are also critical-thinking tests given to those looking to be hired or gain a promotion in the workforce. Some are specific to certain professions, while others are more general and may be used for a wide variety of employment settings. By studying *Critical Thinking Skills Success*, you will be preparing yourself to successfully complete these kinds of exams.

TIP

Remind yourself that you're going to do well on a test before you start. A positive attitude can help you be successful!

Skill Building Until Next Time

- If you are preparing to take an exam that includes a critical thinking skills component, go back to the pretest at the beginning of this book. Which questions did you answer incorrectly? Was there a particular lesson that gave you trouble? Focus your study on those areas.
- Are you in college and planning to enter the workforce? Do some research into the career(s) you are considering. Are there hiring tests given? Most of this information is available on the Internet. Finding out exactly what the test(s) looks like and how it is scored will help you to prepare.

20 ▶ PUTTING IT ALL TOGETHER

*Tell me what you read and I'll tell you who you are is true enough,
but I'd know you better if you told me what you reread.*

François Mauriac, French author (1885–1970)

SUMMARY

You've learned a lot in this book, and this lesson summarizes all the skills covered in Lessons 1–19. Rereading the highlights can help you prepare for the posttest that follows, and can serve as a quick reference any time you're about to take a test at school or for a job. So, keep it handy and reread!

Now that you've arrived at Lesson 20, you may be surprised to find out how much you've learned about critical thinking, so we thought we would summarize. After all, summarizing is an important critical-thinking skill, too. It's important to be able to pick out the main, important ideas in material and present them concisely. You summarize every time you tell someone about a movie you saw, sporting event you attended, or what happened at school or work today. You can't tell everything, minute-by-minute in real time, so you hit the highlights: the main idea and a few details. You can often do it in just a few sentences.

Read over the summaries of the previous 19 lessons on the next few pages to refresh your memory. If anything seems unclear, go back and reread that lesson so you can retain and use all the skills you need for successful critical thinking. Then, keep the book handy as a reference to help you in any future problem-solving situations.

Lesson 1: Recognizing a Problem

You learned that the first step in problem solving is to recognize a situation that needs a solution. Sometimes you find a problem through your own observations, but at other times, someone else tells you about a problem. Next, you prioritize—does the problem need immediate attention, or can it wait? If there's more than one problem, which problem is most important and should be tackled first?

Lesson 2: Defining a Problem

This lesson explained how to avoid "solving" something that is not your actual problem. Defining a real problem entails gathering information and carefully examining what may first appear to be a large problem (it could be a number of smaller ones). It also means not being tricked into solving offshoots of a problem or mistaking the more obvious consequences of a problem for the actual problem. Two ways to be sure you are considering a real problem are to avoid making assumptions and to think the situation through.

Lesson 3: Focused Observation

You learned how to become a more effective decision maker and problem solver by using focused observation.

That means increasing awareness by being thorough, concentrating, and creating a context (looking at a situation as a whole, instead of zeroing in on a small part).

Lesson 4: Brainstorming with Graphic Organizers

In this lesson, you used concept maps, webs, Venn diagrams, charts, and problem/solution outlines to organize your thinking on your way to solutions. Graphic organizers combine text and illustration to show a lot of information in a small space, and keep you focused by showing what you know and what you still need to find out.

Lesson 5: Setting Goals

Here, you learned that goals, the clear statements of what you want to accomplish, should be specific, measurable, realistic, and deadline oriented. If goals are unrealistic, too large, or take too long, they become difficult or impossible to reach, and even if they're reachable, you may grow tired and quit before you get there! Using a goal chart can help keep you on track to meet your goal.

Lesson 6: Troubleshooting

You learned how to troubleshoot problems by thinking ahead, identifying issues that could get in your way, and taking care of them. You also learned about unforeseeable problems, those inconveniences that hold you up as you work toward a goal. Another type of troubleshooting involved problem-causing trends. This must be used when you are consistently faced with the same type of problem, in order to figure out how to prevent it in the future.

Lesson 7: Finding Resources

This lesson stressed getting accurate information. If you have a decision to make, or a problem to solve and you do not know what to base a decision on, or if there are factors that need to be considered that you are not familiar with, you need to consult other resources. They include the Internet, libraries, and experts.

Lesson 8: Evaluating Facts

Here, you learned that a fact is something that can be proven true while an opinion can't. And you discovered the importance of knowing if information is accurate and objective or false and/or biased. To trust any source, you need to check out the author's credentials, documentation and quality of sources, and others' opinions of the source. This is essential, especially when researching on the Internet, where just about anyone can publish and make it seem legitimate.

Lesson 9: Persuasion Techniques

This lesson examined how to recognize persuasion techniques used in speech, writing, and advertising. Three persuasion techniques described by Aristotle thousands of years ago (*logos, pathos, ethos*) are still used today, along with rhetorical questions, hyperboles, and comparisons. These techniques are used in persuasive advertising, where the marketer aims to manipulate your spending habits by making you want to buy his or her product or service. When you understand how persuasion works, you can avoid being swayed by it and use it to your advantage.

Lesson 10: The Numbers Game

You learned how numbers can sometimes lie. Whether by deliberate misuse, negligence, or plain incompetence, the facts and figures we see, hear, and read are not always the truth. It all happens in one, or both, of two key areas. First, numbers must be gathered. If they are collected incorrectly or by someone with an agenda or bias, you need to know that. Second, numbers must be analyzed or interpreted. Again, this process can be done incorrectly, or by an individual or group with an agenda. Surveys, correlation studies, and statistics were examined.

Lesson 11: Checking Your Emotions

This lesson covered the role emotions play in the decision-making process. Emotions and emotional situations explored included bias and stereotypes, stress, and the ego. When emotional responses are recognized and used appropriately they can be an effective component of critical thinking. The goal is to acknowledge and understand the emotions that may influence your decision making, so you can determine when and where to let them become part of the solutions and decisions you make.

Lesson 12: Deductive Reasoning

You learned that in deductive reasoning, an argument is made based on two facts, or premises. These premises could be rules, laws, principles, or generalizations. If they are true, it should follow that the conclusion of the argument must also be true. But, the conclusion must follow logically from and not go beyond or make assumptions about the premises. If it does not, the argument is said to be invalid.

Lesson 13: Errors in Deductive Reasoning

Arguments that have an error in logic, or a fallacy, are invalid. This lesson explored four of the most common logical fallacies: slippery slope, which has true premises but the conclusion takes them to an extreme; false dilemma, which presents only two options (either/or) when there are really more; circular reasoning, which has just one premise, and the conclusion simply restates it; equivocation, which uses a word twice, each time with a different meaning, or one multiple-meaning word that creates ambiguity.

Lesson 14: Inductive Reasoning

This lesson showed how to recognize and construct an inductive argument. Induction is the process of reasoning from the specific (particular facts or instances) to the general (principles, theories, rules). It uses two premises that support the probable truth of the conclusion. To determine what is probable, you must use past experience and/or common sense. The two forms of inductive arguments are comparative (comparing one thing, event or idea to another to see if they are similar), and causal (trying to determine cause from effect).

Lesson 15: Errors in Inductive Reasoning

You learned that an inductive fallacy has either has two premises that don't adequately support the conclusion, or a conclusion that doesn't fit the premises. You explored four common fallacies: hasty generalization, which doesn't have enough evidence in the premises to support the conclusion; chicken-and-egg, which claims cause and effect without enough evidence; *post hoc, ergo propter hoc,* which incorrectly assumes that because one event preceded another, it caused it; and composition, which draws a conclusion based only on the parts of a whole.

Lesson 16: Distracting Techniques

This lesson covered logical fallacies that distract from the real issue, putting an opponent on the defensive. Three such techniques are: red herring, in which the opponent of an argument throws in an irrelevant topic to change the subject to one with which he or she is more comfortable; straw man, which distracts from the original argument by creating a weaker one that is easier to attack; and *ad hominem*, which attacks the opponent instead of the issue.

Lesson 17: Making Judgment Calls

You learned that judgment calls are subjective, debatable decisions that have four characteristics: the stakes are high, needed information is incomplete or ambiguous, other people disagree about them, and they sometimes involve conflicting values. It's necessary to always take the time to evaluate all the risks and weigh the consequences of each possible decision.

Lesson 18: Explanation or Argument?

You learned that an explanation is made up of two parts: the *explanadum*, what will be explained; and the *explanans*, the statements that do the explaining. A good explanation gives new information, the topic is accepted as fact, it's relevant, and when accepted, removes or lessens a problem. An explanation answers the question, "why?" An argument, on the other hand, gives reasons (premises) that are evidence for a conclusion and may be opinions or value judgments. Explanations are neither of those.

Lesson 19: Critical Thinking for Exams

In this lesson, you discovered how to use the skills you learned in *Critical Thinking Skills Success in 20 Minutes a Day* when you take exams to get into colleges or grad schools or to get a job. Critical reading questions on tests measure your ability to understand a passage, draw inferences, analyze information, and critique others peoples' arguments. Other tests measure science reasoning, analytical writing, and logical and situational reasoning. Lesson 19 explained which skills can help you best answer questions on these tests correctly.

TIP

Summarize each lesson in this book yourself. Draw a triangle and write the three most important facts, one in each corner. Use this technique with everything you read to help you help you remember what you read and increase your critical-thinking skills!

Practice

Here are a few questions about the summaries.

1. A summary is always
   a. supposed to be amusing.
   b. include as many details as possible.
   c. shorter than the original material.
   d. supposed to identify only the opinions of the writer.

2. Problem solving begins with
   a. carefully constructing a survey.
   b. researching an answer.
   c. making a deductive evaluation.
   d. identifying an actual problem that needs solving.

3. A graphic organizer
   a. is only helpful for showing statistics, as on a graph.
   b. combines words and visuals so you can see information at a glance.
   c. isn't as helpful as writing an essay about a problem.
   d. can interfere with logical thinking as you search for a solution.

4. A clear statement of what someone wants to accomplish is
   a. an intuition.
   b. a deductive reason.
   c. a goal.
   d. an observation.

5. Thinking ahead about something that might impede solving a problem is called
   a. forbearance.
   b. tolerance.
   c. bias.
   d. troubleshooting.

6. A fact is
  a. something that can be proven to be true.
  b. anything defined as "fictional material."
  c. something that can be believed only if read on the Internet.
  d. anything someone else tells you.

7. Which does NOT define a fallacy?
  a. false impression
  b. mistake in logic
  c. apprehension
  d. erroneous belief

Answers

1. c, **2.** d, **3.** b, **4.** c, **5.** d, **6.** a, **7.** c.

In Short

Now that you have reviewed each of the lessons, it is time to test your skills with the posttest. Use this posttest to determine your improvement since the pretest and to see what weaknesses remain.

POSTTEST

Now that you've completed the 20 lessons in *Critical Thinking Skills Success in 20 Minutes a Day*, it's time to find out how much you've improved! The 30 questions on this posttest are similar to those on the pretest, that way you can compare your knowledge before and after completing the book. In addition, this test includes some vocabulary covered in the lessons, but not used in the pretest.

If this is your book, circle the correct answers to multiple-choice questions and write your longer answers directly on the test pages. If the book isn't yours, list the numbers 1–30 on a piece of paper and write your answers to all the questions there. Take as much time as you need, and then review the answer explanations on pages 163–164. They include the lesson number the question relates to. So if you answer any question incorrectly, check out that lesson to refresh your memory. Good luck!

1. You arrange a job interview for Monday morning. When you arrive at the office, the interviewer is not there. You wait for 20 minutes, but he does not show up. What pieces of information can help you create a context for this problem? (circle all that apply)
   a. You heard a traffic report about a tie-up on the interstate.
   b. You realize you forgot your resume, and need to go home to get it.
   c. The interviewer's secretary tells you the interview is on the calendar for Tuesday.
   d. The receptionist makes a comment about how the interviewer is not punctual.

2. Three problems arise at work simultaneously. In what order should you solve the following:
   a. A package must be shipped to your west coast office by 4:00.
   b. Your boss needs a report on profit projections for a 1:00 meeting.
   c. You accidentally delete the computer file containing the rough draft of the profit report.

3. Which rhetorical devices are used in the following? (choose all that apply)
   "The Civil War was the darkest moment in human history. From bloody battlefields to brothers caught in bitter brawls, over half a million lost their lives. They fought over slavery, economics, and the very Constitution itself. Is it any wonder this sad episode in American history still fascinates?"
   a. comparison
   b. rhetorical question
   c. sound pattern
   d. hyperbole

4. Which statement is NOT an example of bias or stereotyping?
   a. I told Blair she needs a lawyer, but she refuses. She said they only care about making money for themselves.
   b. Todd said Ruth was promoted instead of him because she's a beautiful woman.
   c. I can't believe I got the lead in the school play. The guess I did okay at the audition!
   d. Nancy won't date anyone who hasn't graduated from an Ivy League school.

5. Which explains the following statement?
   "If you do not start exercising, you will get heart disease."
   a. It appeals to the senses.
   b. It is an example of the logical fallacy called false dilemma.
   c. It is a true statement even though it sounds drastic.
   d. It is an example of the logical fallacy called *post hoc ergo propter hoc.*

6. Which is probably a personal web page?
   a. www.members.aol.com/pspeabody63/
   b. www.stateuniversity.edu
   c. www.fastfacts.com
   d. www.veteransunite.org

7. Steve has an unexpected emergency. He needs to fly to Seattle because his grandfather is in the hospital. Steve knows he'll be away from his apartment for at least three weeks. How can he troubleshoot problems that could occur while he's gone? (Circle all answers that apply.)
a. Buy a new lock for his door.
b. Leave a mail key with a neighbor who can collect Steve's mail so it doesn't pile up.
c. Ask a friend who's an animal lover to care for his two cats.
d. Clean out the refrigerator so food doesn't go bad before he returns.

8. Which is NOT a valid deductive argument?
a. All the people at my party work in my department at the company. If Ross is at my party, then Ross must work in my department.
b. When I wear red I think I look heavier. I'll wear this blue dress tonight. Therefore, I'll look really skinny.
c. I'm can't eat shellfish because of my allergies. Shrimp are shellfish, so I can't eat these shrimp.
d. I like all of Leonardo daVinci's paintings. He painted the *Mona Lisa*. Therefore, I like the *Mona Lisa*.

9. Why is the following statement NOT an example of problem solving?
  "The teacher gave me a low grade on my project because he's unhappy at home."
a. because the speaker doesn't know how to cheer up the teacher
b. because the speaker is just angry about getting a lower than expected grade
c. because the speaker thinks the project was better than it really was
d. because the speaker is making an assumption about the teacher that might not be true

Read the following passage, and answer questions 10 and 11.

One of the major causes of the French Revolution of 1789 was the social class system. The population was divided into three Estates, with the clergy, the monarchy, and noblemen in the top two, and peasants and the middle class in the third. Clergy and noblemen were not required to pay taxes, and had representation in the government. The monarchy lived lavishly and led a repressive regime that silenced its critics. The bourgeoisie paid heavy taxes, had no representation in the government, and resented the King's power and excesses. They grew angry at the unjust system, and finally revolted by storming the Bastille, a state prison in Paris.

10. What did the Bastille represent to the Third Estate?
a. the place of last resort
b. the excesses of the big city
c. the unjust, repressive government
d. the First and Second Estates

11. In France's three Estates of social class, the top two included the
- **a.** clergy, noblemen, and middle class.
- **b.** clergy, monarchy, and noblemen.
- **c.** monarchy, noblemen, and middle class.
- **d.** clergy, middle class, and peasants.

12. Ramona is unhappy in her current job and wants to find a new one. What is a realistic goal for her job search?
- **a.** "I want a new job by next month. I will read the classifieds for the next four weeks, answer all interesting ads the day I see them, and line up interviews when I get responses."
- **b.** "I want a new job by next month. I will update my resume, and send it out to every company I am interested in working for. I will follow up the mailing with phone calls until I get an interview."
- **c.** "I want a new job within the next few months. This week, I will work on my resume. For the next three weeks, I will research other companies. Then, I will start networking. With the contact information I get, I will send out my resumes."
- **d.** "I want a new job within the next year. I will do some networking, especially with my alumni organization. I will update my resume, and do some cold calling to see if there are any openings for someone with my skills and experience."

13. Which is NOT an example of *post hoc* reasoning?
- **a.** It always rains the same day I wash my car!
- **b.** Reba had eggs for breakfast and got a phone call that she won money.
- **c.** Tito's soccer team won every time he remembered to carry his lucky penny.
- **d.** Our band started playing more gigs after we advertised in the local paper.

14. You are assigned a paper on a current political topic, and your professor stresses that it must be balanced and objective. How can you evaluate the sources you find in the course of your research? (choose all that apply)
- **a.** Find out the author's credentials.
- **b.** Look for web pages written by individuals who seem to have done a lot of research on the topic.
- **c.** Check for statistical information.
- **d.** Check the author's sources to see if they are reputable.

15. You are considering accepting a job offer in another state, 400 miles away. List four problems you might encounter if you move. Brainstorm two possible solutions for each problem.

Problem 1: _____

    Solution 1: _____

    Solution 2: _____

Problem 2: _____

    Solution 1: _____

    Solution 2: _____

Problem 3: _____

    Solution 1: _____

    Solution 2: _____

Problem 4: _____

    Solution 1: _____

    Solution 2: _____

16. What problems will most likely result from the following scenario?

Because of rising health insurance costs for government workers, there is a budget crisis in your state. The governor vowed not to raise taxes, so she is making drastic cuts in services to balance the budget. The biggest cuts are to the Department of Transportation, which is getting just 50% of its projected needs.

_____

_____

_____

_____

17. What two things are wrong with the following survey?

An environmental group sent out a questionnaire to 500 of its members. It began with an introduction about how local politicians are making it easier for developers to get permits to build in designated wetlands areas. Then they asked, "Do you think our precious natural resources, such as wetlands, should be depleted, so a handful of developers can get richer?"

a. The population is not random—the questionnaire was only sent to group's members.

b. The margin of error is too high.

c. The population is too large.

d. The question is biased—"precious" and "get richer" indicate the author's subjective intent.

18. Which is an example of an unfinished claim?

a. Only sensitive, intelligent people use Taupe Soap.

b. Buy our ground beef—it is fresher and better tasting.

c. Big Bob's Music World has the lowest prices on the hottest CDs.

d. Stand out in a crowd! Wear LookAtMe perfume.

19. Your company has just moved its offices to a new building. There is a group of parking spaces designated for your company, but there are not enough spaces for everyone, and you must sometimes pay to park on the street. What is the best, most time-effective way to find out how to solve this problem?

a. Write a letter to the property management company.

b. Ask your personnel manager to look into the situation for you.

c. Send an e-mail to your boss explaining the problem.

d. Call the owner of the building.

20. Which word in each example is the equivocation?

a. Pools are full of water, so car pools must be pretty wet rides.

b. If everything is relative, then why aren't we related?

c. This pasta sauce can't be light. It weighs just as much as a regular pasta sauce!

d. This website is devoted to some really odd things. You are 21, so you should be mentioned on this website.

21. What is the best conclusion for the following inductive argument?

The last time we went up against this defense team, they had no concrete evidence, but they produced 150 boxes of documents. We wasted countless hours looking through them. For this case, we just got a truckload of documents. We should probably

a. read through every single sheet of paper, and document them, just in case.

b. assign a few paralegals to go through a random selection of boxes to see if there is anything worthwhile.

c. forget about them. There is probably nothing we need in those documents.

d. look at the top document in each box to see if it could be of use to our case.

22. Keela was assigned a term paper on the Hubble Space Telescope. She wants to find information on the federal funding of the telescope. Which website should she use to find this information?

a. http://hubble.nasa.gov

b. www.mindspring.com/~deline/

c. www.pbs.org/deepspace/hubble/

d. www.thehubbletelescope.com

23. Read the following, and then answer the question:
"I went to a pool party once and there was a terrible accident," Alexis said. "This one girl slipped, hit her head on the edge of the pool, and was hospitalized with a concussion! I'll never go to a pool party again!"
Alexis' assertion is an example of
  a. a well-founded conclusion.
  b. a hasty generalization.
  c. an opinion that's valid.
  d. circular reasoning.

24. What are four qualities of a valuable goal?
  a. written down, specific, measurable, told to a friend
  b. specific, measurable, realistic, honorable
  c. written down, realistic, deadline oriented, challenging
  d. specific, measurable, realistic, deadline oriented

25. Why is the following a poor judgment call?
During an audition for a new theater group, Gigi had a feeling the group president, Matthew, didn't like her. When he invited her to be part of the group and offered her a part in the first production, she turned him down. *Why would I want to be around people who don't like me?* she thought.
  a. Gigi is unreasonable; she can't know for sure if Matthew liked her or not. And who cares, he obviously liked her work!
  b. Gigi should take the part in the play to prove what a good actress she is.
  c. Gigi is obviously jealous of Matthew because he is head of the group.
  d. Gigi should rely on real facts, not just a hunch that someone doesn't like her, before deciding whether to join the acting group.

26. Which is the best conclusion for the following argument?
Every store in Madison Mall is having a 60% off sale on Thursday. Faye's Fashions is in Madison Mall. Therefore,
  a. prices were lower at Faye's Fashions yesterday.
  b. on Thursday, Faye's Fashions is having a 60% off sale.
  c. prices at Madison Mall are lower than at Midtown Mall.
  d. on Thursday, prices at the mall will be 20% less than today.

27. While (**T**) true or (**F**) false for each of the following statements.
  ____ **a.** Internet search engines lead you only to the best sites about the subject you are researching.
  ____ **b.** Some Internet sites cost money to search with full access.
  ____ **c.** Subject directories are sometimes written by experts in their fields.
  ____ **d.** Information on websites is just as reliable as information found in libraries.

28. Label each statement as an (**A**) argument or an (**E**) explanation.
  ____ **a.** There must be something wrong with the modem, because this computer doesn't work.
  ____ **b.** Gina was late to the party because she missed her train.
  ____ **c.** All schools should have vending machines that dispense apples, other fruit, and granola snacks because experts say most kids don't get enough healthy food at home.
  ____ **d.** Israel's going to California because he's starting at UCLA next month.

29. What is wrong with the following statement?
We would all benefit if we joined the union. They get salaries of up to $40,000, double pay for overtime, and $15 deductibles on health insurance policies for their workers.

a. Workers are rarely better off when they join a union.

b. The union is asking for too much from management and probably won't get it.

c. We don't know if the union gets double pay for overtime for everyone, or just some workers.

d. We don't know what the workers have already in terms of salary, overtime pay, and deductibles.

30. Identify each *ad hominem* fallacy as (**A**) abusive, (**C**) circumstantial, or (**TQ**) *tu quoque*.

___ **a.** Of course he is against gun control. He works for a rifle manufacturer.

___ **b.** I thought you said borrowing money was a bad idea. Now you are taking out a car loan? I guess you were wrong—borrowing money is a great idea.

___ **c.** My boss is so cheap. I have been working for her for six months and I still haven't gotten a raise!

___ **d.** Did you buy that children's book on morals? I heard the writer got charged with drunk driving. How can her book be anything but hypocritical garbage?

Answers

1. Choices **a**, **c**, and **d** could all create a context for the problem. Choice **b** is irrelevant. (Lesson 3)

2. The order that makes the most sense is **c**, **b**, **a**. The report is needed soonest, but the deleted file must be retrieved or rewritten before it can be delivered. The package can wait until after the report is delivered. (Lesson 1)

3. Choices **b** (*sad episode*), **c** (*bloody battlefields to brothers caught in bitter brawls*), and **d** (*darkest moment in human history*) are correct. (Lesson 9)

4. Choice **c** has no bias or stereotyping. The speaker's remarks don't influence anyone's ideas or behavior. (Lesson 11)

5. Choice **b** is a false dilemma because it reduces the number of options to one, when in fact there are others. Many people who do not exercise never develop heart disease. (Lesson 13)

6. Choice **a** is most likely a personal web page. (Lesson 8)

7. Choices **b**, **c**, and **d** make sense, but there's no reason to get a new lock if the old one isn't broken. (Lesson 6)

8. Choice **b** isn't valid because its major premise, that red makes me look heavier, isn't addressed in the conclusion; we can't conclude that blue or any color can make me look really skinny. (Lesson 12)

9. The best answer is **d**. Assumptions have no place in effective problem solving. (Lesson 2)

10. The answer is **c**. As a State prison, the Bastille represented the government's oppression. (Lesson 19)

11. The answer is choice **b**. (Lesson 19)

12. Choice **c** is the most realistic goal. Some goals should be deadline oriented, so even though Ramona is realistic about her job search taking up to a year, she sets smaller goals, such as updating her resume in a week and doing research for three weeks. (Lesson 5)

13. Choice **d** isn't an example of *post hoc* reasoning; The ads actually did cause the band to get more jobs. (Lesson 15)

14. Choices **a**, **b**, and **d** are all important. Individuals' web pages, while they may look professional, can be bogus, and they may not be reliable sources of information. (Lesson 8)

15. Problems and solutions may vary. Some possible answers:

Problem 1—too far away from family

Solution 1: plan regular visits

Solution 2: schedule weekly phone calls

Problem 2—have to sell house and find a new place to live

Solution 1: set up meeting with local realtors

Solution 2: run ads in local papers

Problem 3—don't know way around new city

Solution 1: go online to city government site for information and maps

Solution 2: get information from personnel office

Problem 4—children have to go to a new school

Solution 1: get records from current school

Solution 2: find new neighborhood kids to help your kids adjust (Lesson 4)

16. Answers should include reduction or elimination of services provided by the Department of Transportation, such as bus and train service, road maintenance, bridge and tunnel repairs, and highway rest stops. (Lesson 2)

17. Choices **a** and **d** are correct. The population is not random if it was sent only to the group's members, and the words "precious" and "get richer" indicate the author's subjective, biased intent. (Lesson 10)

18. The answer is choice **b**. It stops short of telling you what it is fresher and better tasting than. (Lesson 9)

19. Choice **b** is the best answer. Sending a letter and waiting for a reply could take a week or more. A personnel manager probably has frequent contact with the person or people who can help you. (Lesson 7)

20. Choice **a**, "pool." Choice **b**, "relative." Choice **c**, "light." Choice **d**, "odd." The fallacy of equivocation occurs when two meanings of a word are used or implied within the same argument. (Lesson 13)

21. Choice **b** is the best answer, because even though there is reason to believe there is nothing of value in the documents, the stakes are typically high in a lawsuit, and it is worth a look to see if any thing of importance was produced. (Lesson 14)

22. Choice **a** is the best answer since the government website most likely has details about the funding of the Hubble. Choice **b** is a personal web page, and although choices **c** and **d** are about Hubble, they probably don't include information about on-going funding for the project. (Lesson 8)

23. The answer is choice **b**. (Lesson 15)

24. The answer is **d**. A goal doesn't have to be told to a friend (choice **a**), honorable (choice **b**), or challenging (choice **c**). (Lesson 5)

25. The answer is choice **d**. Hunches alone should never be used to make a judgment. (Lesson 17)

26. The answer is **b**; a conclusion must include information from the premise (every store is having a 60% off sale). (Lesson 12).

27. **a**, false (search engines show "hits," not necessarily the best sites); **b**, true; **c**, true; **d**, false (be more suspicious because just about anyone can create a website). (Lesson 7)

28. Choice **a** is an explanation. Choice **b** is argument. Choice **c** is an argument. Choice **d** is an explanation. (Lesson 18)

29. Choice **d** is the correct answer. There is too much information left out to know if what the union wants for the workers is any better than what they already have. (Lesson 10)

30. a. circumstantial, working for a gun manufacturer might not be why he's against gun control; **b.** *tu quoque*, just because the action goes against the statement doesn't make the statement wrong; **c.** abusive, not getting a raise doesn't always mean a boss is cheap; **d.** *tu quoque*, the crime doesn't mean the book is garbage. (Lesson 15)

GLOSSARY

ad hominem   attack on the person making an argument rather than on the argument itself

analyze   clarify information by examining parts and relationships

argument   tells how we know something

bias   preferences or beliefs that make one unfair or partial

brainstorm   come up with as many ideas as possible

classify   group items by common attributes

compare   look for ways things are alike

conclusion   a decision based on given facts and inferences

contrast   look for ways things are different

criteria   set of standards or conditions to be met

critical thinking   focus on making decisions about what to do or believe

decision making   selecting from among possible choices

deductive reasoning   concludes that something must be true because it's a special case of a law, rule, or a widely accepted principle

emotions   feelings, sentiments

equivocation   use or imply two meanings for a word within the same argument

ethos   persuasion appealing to character

evaluate   assess suitability and quality of an idea, action, or object

explanandum   something that will be explained

explanans   statements that explain

explanation   tells why something is so

fact   something that can be proven to be true
fallacy   erroneous belief or myth

glittering generalities   propaganda that appeals to the emotions
goal   clear statement of something one wants to accomplish in the future
graphic organizer   art and text used to organize information so it can be used effectively

hyperbole   exaggeration used to make a point

inductive reasoning   assumes that a general principle is true because of special cases that have been true
inference   a logical guess based on facts and personal experiences

judgment call   decision made when there is not enough evidence for a right or wrong answer

logos   persuasion that appeals to reason

metacognition   awareness and control of one's thinking

name calling   insulting or sarcastic language with negative connotations

observe   gather information using one or more senses
opinion   what someone thinks; can't be proven true or false

pathos   persuasion appealing to emotions
persuasion   the ability to influence how people think or act
post hoc **reasoning**   false argument that because one thing precedes another, it causes it
prediction   an educated guess about what will happen in the future
prior knowledge   information learned previously on a topic
prioritize   rank projects or goals by importance of competition
problem   a question or situation that calls for a solution
propaganda   the spreading of ideas to influence the opinions or behavior of others

red herring   something that diverts attention away from the real issue
resources   books and other materials used for research
rhetorical question   implies the answer is obvious and one has no choice but to agree

solution   resolution of a problem
statistics   collection of measurable data
stereotyping   generalized or prejudiced opinions about a group of people
straw man   unrelated topic brought into an argument to divert attention
summarize   combine all pertinent information into a cohesive statement

troubleshoot   identify possible problems and find solutions for them before they occur

valid   authentic, well founded
verify   confirm the accuracy, truth, or quality of an observation or data